Supply Chain Roadmap

Supply Chain Roadmap

aligning supply chain with business strategy

Hernan David Perez

Copyright © 2013 Hernan David Perez

All rights reserved. No part of this publication may be reproduced or transmitted or distributed in any form or by any means -*electronic, mechanical, photocopying, recording, broadcast, or otherwise*- or stored in a database or retrieval system, without the prior written consent of the proprietary of the copyright, including, but no limited to, in any network or other electronic storage or transmission, or broadcast for distance learning.

ISBN: 149420049X
ISBN-13: 978-1494200497

Preface

Why so often does it seem that a company is on one path and its supply chain is on another path?

Answering this question is difficult, partly because it sounds illogical and partly because it is not easy to understand why the supply chain and the business strategy are so often misaligned.

In pursuit of the answer to these questions, I searched about existing theory in supply chain strategy, and I found several very good developed theories. But they were eminently conceptual, hindering their application in business cases. Consequently, I searched for methods that would allow the assessment of the supply chain strategy, but again, the findings were very few, and in many cases restricted to hiring large consulting companies.

Definitively, there was an opportunity to develop a simple method that would allow for the understanding, evaluating, and reformulating of the supply chain strategy of organizations; a method that would be equivalent to what is the balanced scorecard and the blue ocean strategy to business strategy.

For the past three years, I have spent much of my time working on this project, exchanging points of view with people around the world, exposing the method in different forums. This is the moment to share the method with all supply chain people: students, professors, professionals, consultants and industries related to supply chain management.

The book is organized in three sections:

Section 1: Introduction, in which concepts about strategy and supply chain and the theoretical fundamentals behind the Supply Chain Roadmap method are explained: the three perspectives of the supply chain strategy (Business Framework, Unique Value Proposal, and Supply Chain Processes).

Section 2: Supply Chain Roadmap Tools, in which the four tools used for applying the method are explained: The Map, 10-Common-Patterns, 6 Supply Chain Archetypes, and the Feasibility Matrix.

Section 3: Applying the method, in which the 4-Steps method is presented. This method is a step-by-step method allowing for the application of the Supply Chain Roadmap method to real cases; in addition to above, three cases of application of the Supply Chain Roadmap method are presented.

Contents

Preface 5

Contents 7

SECTION 1: Introduction 11

    Introduction to Supply Chain Strategy 14

        Supply Chain Management 14

        What Is Strategy? 16

        What Is Operations Strategy? 18

        From Operations Strategy to Supply Chain Strategy 19

    Theory behind Supply Chain Roadmap method 22

        Three Perspectives for Formulating Supply Chain Strategy 22

            Business Framework 23

            Unique Value Proposal 24

            Supply Chain Processes 27

        The Map 28

SECTION 2: Tools of the Supply Chain Roadmap 31

    Tool 1: The Map 34

        Business Framework Perspective 36

            Sourcing View 36

            Technology View 39

            Demand View 42

        Unique Value Proposal Perspective 46

            Product Attributes 47

            Service Attributes 48

        Supply Chain Processes Perspective 50

            Sourcing Process 50

            Plan and Make Processes 53

    Demand Fulfillment Process 59
    Managerial Focus 63

Tool 2: 10 Common Patterns 72
  Common Pattern 1: Industries in a Low-Challenging Sourcing Pattern 73
  Common Pattern 2: Industries in a High-Challenging Sourcing Position 74
  Common Pattern 3: "Commoditized" Industries 76
  Common Pattern 4: "Evolving" Industries 78
  Common Pattern 5: UVP Geared to Low Inventory 79
  Common Pattern 6: UVP Geared to Perfect Orders 80
  Common Pattern 7: UVP Offers a Broad Portfolio 82
  Common Pattern 8: UVP Offers Short Lead Times 83
  Common Pattern 9: High Relevance of Transport Costs 84
  Common Pattern 10: Evolving Portfolio 86

Tool 3: Supply Chain Archetypes 90
  Supply Chain Archetypes Driven by Efficiency 90
    The Efficient Supply Chain Archetype 91
    The "Fast" Supply Chain Archetype 97
    The "Continuous Flow" Supply Chain Archetype 102
    Comparison of Supply Chains Oriented to Efficiency 107
  Supply Chains Oriented to Responsiveness 109
    The Agile Supply Chain Archetype 110
    The Custom-Configured Supply Chain Archetype 115
    The Flexible Supply Chain 121
    Comparison of Supply Chains Oriented to Responsiveness 126

Tool 4: Feasibility Matrix 130

SECTION 3: Applying the Method 133
  Supply Chain Roadmap's Four-Step Method 136
    Step 1: Scope 137
    Step 2: Understanding 140
    Step 3: Evaluation 144
      Selecting the Best Suited Supply Chain Archetype 145
      Evolution Gaps 148

  Design Gaps 149
  Compliance Gaps 151
 Step 4: Redesign & Deployment 153
Applying the Supply Chain Roadmap 158
 Alpha: A Manufacturer of Intermediate Goods for the Textile Industry 160
  Step 1: Segmentation 160
  Step 2: Understanding 160
  Step 3: Evaluation 164
  Step 4: Redesign & Deployment 173
  Results 176
 CROCS: When Strategy and Implementation Are Misaligned 177
 Tamago Ya: When a Focused Supply Chain Creates an Unmatched Value Proposal ... 180

Outlook 185

About the author 185

Notes and references 186

SECTION 1: Introduction

In the past twenty years, business strategy has been demystified through the contribution of several methods like Balanced Scorecard from Kaplan & Norton, Blue Ocean Strategy from Kim and Mauborgne, Delta Model from Arnoldo Hax, and most recently, Business Generation Model from Osterwalder and Pigneur. These methods have been available to organizations, which have assimilated this knowledge and put it into the planning processes of the business strategy.

Supply chain strategy was born in 1997 in the article "What is the right supply chain for your product?" by Marshall Fisher, and from that arose different approaches and theories around supply chain strategy. However, these theoretical approaches to formulating and validating supply chain strategy have not had the same success as the methods for formulating the business strategy. This is largely because they have not paid enough attention to the connections and combinations among key drivers throughout the value chain, or to their alignment with the framework of industry and with an organization's competitive positioning.

In order to address these shortcomings, I have conducted an analysis of the most widely recognized theories and case studies about supply chain strategy. My analysis has identified a set of common configurations that reveal key drivers of supply chain strategy and explains how these can be aligned in a coherent strategy. These findings are summarized in a strategy formulation model called the Supply Chain Roadmap ®, which provides:

A compilation of the most relevant key drivers of a supply chain strategy

An understanding of the interrelation between these key drivers and an industry's competitive framework as well as a business's competitive positioning

The characteristic profile of six Supply Chain Archetypes: efficient, fast, continuous-flow, agile, custom-configured, and flexible

The Supply Chain Roadmap is not a new type of supply chain strategy. Rather, the Supply Chain Roadmap method is supported in the most important and recognized theories and practices about supply chain strategy and business strategy, such as the contributions of Michael Porter, Kaplan & Norton, Arnoldo Hax, Marshall Fisher, John Gattorna, AT Kearney, Martin Christopher, Hau Lee, and Terry Hill among others.

The Supply Chain Roadmap contribution resides in the development of a simple method to identify the relevance of a supply chain strategy within an organization's Business Framework through a four-step method. Those four steps are:
- Scope
- Understand
- Evaluate
- Redesign

The Supply Chain Roadmap is not a quantitative method with a unique or predefined solution. Rather, it is a method whereby an organization's supply chain strategy can be reviewed in an organized and systematic approach in order to assure alignment of the supply chain with the business strategy.

Chapter 01
Introduction

What is this thing called Supply Chain?

Introduction to Supply Chain Strategy

Supply Chain Management

In 1982, the term "Supply Chain Management" was coined by Keith Oliver, senior vice president of Booz Allen Hamilton (now Booz & Company), in an interview with the Financial Times. Some years later, in 2003, Oliver explained the "Total Supply Chain Management" concept[i], as the development of a function responsible in the end to end of the organization for the reduction in inventory and a simultaneous improvement in customer service, tearing down the functional silos separating the traditional processes—*marketing, sales, production, distribution, and finance*—into the organizations.

The supply chain concept was revolutionary for its time, and it took some time for organizations to consider and introduce it into the organization's strategy. Some years later, in 1985, Michael Porter introduced the terms "Value Chain" and "Value System"[ii], which described the interaction among firms and their suppliers and customers as well as the connections among the functions of the company. Porter's concepts were similar to the supply chain concept developed by Oliver some years before. In 1993, Hammer & Champy introduced "Reengineering the Corporation," which again advocated defragmenting and moving functions to process thinking, again, similar to the statement by Oliver in the 1980s.

As they say, necessity is the mother of invention, and supply chain became important in the 1990s and early 2000s, when industries faced fierce competition scaled to levels unimaginable years earlier, due to factors such as product technological maturity, a greater number of competitors in the market, free trade agreements, the advantage of scale of competitors with global reach, offshore manufacturing, information technology revolution, and a more demanding customer in terms of cost, innovation, and response time. Consequently, the supply chain function became a key element used by organizations to compete and differentiate themselves in the markets. Because the supply chain orchestrates the flow of information, products, and money from suppliers—*from the manufacturing phase to the transformation process to customers*—it strongly affects an organization's competitiveness in factors such as product cost, working capital, the speed at which it reaches the market, and service perception, among other issues.

Despite the massive introduction of supply chain function into the organizations, confusion persists about its meaning. The confusion rests in the conceptual differences among the different approaches for defining supply chain management (SCM). According to Mentzer,[iii] three main approaches define supply chain:

SCM is a set of activities geared toward implementing a management philosophy. This approach is focused on defining the corporate competencies that companies must develop in order to operate a competitive supply chain.

SCM is a process management tool. The synchronization of business functions is geared toward the management of cash flow, materials, and information from suppliers to customers, and is focused on fulfilling a customer's requirement.

SCM is a management philosophy. SCM is a competitive strategy, whereby companies create connections throughout its supply chain, enhancing and optimizing efforts so as to create differentiated value proposals.

The first two approaches focus on defining SCM in tactical terms, while the notion of SCM as a management philosophy focuses on defining the orientation and strategic approach of the company's supply chain. Based on the Mentzer's approach to define Supply Chain as a management philosophy, I propose a definition of supply chain, as *is shown in* Figure 1.1.

> **Supply chain is the business function responsible for the connection and combination of activities related to the management within and among organizations of the flow of:**
> - **Materials and Products**
> - **Information**
> - **Commercial and financial transactions**
>
> **Aiming to achieve a unique combination of perceived value for the customer in the competitive environment in which the company operates**

Figure 1.1 Supply Chain Definition

What Is Strategy?

In his well-known article "What is strategy?"[iv] Michael Porter argues that, "Competitive strategy consists in being different. It means deliberately choosing a set of different activities in order to provide a unique combination of value." It is this unique combination of value that constitutes an organization's strategic positioning, which is based on a mix of three facets of positioning: variety, needs, and access.

Positioning based on variety, in which the source of value is concentrated in offering a supply of products or services for different customer segments, is considered appropriate when an organization can produce products or services better than its competitors, even though it probably cannot satisfy all the needs of a specific group of customers.

Positioning based on needs is present when the source of value is concentrated on attending to the largest portion of needs of a specific group of customers.

Positioning based on access can be offered when the manner of accessing customers is unique, even if the needs of a group of customers are similar.

The focus of these three positions is a more advanced approach of the generic strategies presented by Porter in 1985, which represented three basic strategic positioning approaches: leadership in costs, differentiation, and access.

Strategy does not end with the definition of the strategic positioning, since it is necessary to define the manner in which the activities and functions inside the organization are articulated by means of a "fit." The fit defines the manner in which activities connect, complement, and reinforce among them. The fit is, in a few words, the assurance of the business's alignment from top to bottom, including outside the organization's limits, working in a collaborative way with suppliers and customers. Porter defines three types of fit: simple compatibility, enhanced compatibility, and effort optimization.

Simple compatibility is evident when the competitive advantages of the organization's activities and functions accumulate throughout the value chain, such as, for example, in an organization that is focused on a cost-based leadership strategy based on the reduction of costs in each one of the individual activities.

Enhanced compatibility is demonstrated when the competitive advantages of the organization's activities and functions mutually reinforce themselves, generating added value and competitive advantage that are greater than the sum of the organization's individual competitive advantages. For example, an organization geared toward a cost-based leadership strategy, ensuring that all the processes and activities are geared toward low-cost production, and, in addition to above, the activities within a process reinforce the strategy in activities that come before or after the value chain. Following this example, product design is focused not only on generating cost savings within the activity in itself, but also on having manufacturing and distribution operations reduce cost due to an optimized product design as well as to individual improvement activities in each one of these areas.

Effort optimization occurs when redundancies are eliminated and waste is minimized in activities and functions throughout the value chain, supported in both internal activities and activities carried out by the members of the value network. For example, an organization focused on a rapid response to the market, which administers the unified inventory of the entire network, with the purpose of minimizing arrival time to the consumer and optimizing operative and capital costs associated to excess inventory in the chain.

The sustainability of strategic positioning is stronger when the fit of the activities and functions throughout the value network is founded on enhanced compatibility and/or effort optimization connections, since these connections are more difficult for competitors to interpret and replicate.

Finally, rephrasing Porter, we can conclude that: *While operative efficacy deals with reaching excellence in individual activities or functions, the strategy is in charge of defining the connection and combination of activities and functions throughout the value chain, in order to achieve a unique combination of value under Customer's perception.*

What Is Operations Strategy?

Wickham Skinner, one of the most renowned authors in topics concerning operations strategy, in his article "The Productivity Paradox"[v] defines operations strategy as *"the required competitive leverage and made possible by the production function, in order to produce structural definitions such as: Buying or Doing, installed capacity, manufacturing network, process technology, quality assurance system, information systems, policies involving the administration of the work force and organizational structure."*

Terry Hill, another prominent author in operations strategy, makes an additional and significant contribution, when he introduces the concepts of *"Order Winners"* and *"Order Qualifiers"* so as to ensure an operations strategy oriented toward the market, and that in Hill's words *"creates the essential interface between marketing and operations in order to understand markets from the point of view of both functions ... Helping companies move from the vague understanding of the market to a new, essential level of knowledge."*[vi]

While Hill emphasizes the alignment of the operations strategy with market requirements, Skinner defines the structural elements that comprise the operations strategy in a precise manner, both of them constituting complementary approaches regarding the operations strategy, and both definitions giving the first approaches to what later became known as supply chain management.

From Operations Strategy to Supply Chain Strategy

The first widely recognized proposal of a segmented model for a supply chain strategy arises from Fisher (1997)[vii], who in his classic article "What Is the Right Supply Chain for Your Product?" suggests that the design of the supply chain must be defined with respect to the product type. For functional products, he recommends efficient supply chains, and for innovative products, he recommends agile supply chains.

Martin Christopher (2000, 2006)[viii] adds the lead-time criteria to Fisher's product type criteria for the selection of the supply chain model by developing a 2x2 matrix and introduces agile, lean, and lean agile supply chain concepts.

Alongside, Lee (2002)[ix] develops the "uncertainty framework" concept, in which starting from the interaction between the uncertainty of demand and the uncertainty of sourcing, he introduces four types of supply chains as follows: efficient, agile, rapid response, and risk coverage.

Later, Christopher and Gattorna (2005)[x] define the concept of "alignment of supply chains with the Customer's needs" and introduce four generic supply chains: collaborative, efficient, rapid response, and innovative.

Gattorna (2006)[xi] subsequently evolved this concept to "dynamic supply chains," in which he presents four types of supply chains: agile, efficient, continuous replenishment, and flexible. In the interim, the "Best Value Supply Chain" (Ketchen & Hult 2007)[xii] arose, which is a hybrid approach combining elements of the generic chains proposed previously by other authors.

It is important to highlight that these authors use similar terminology for naming the generic supply chains, but they develop different concepts in the modus operandi and in these generic chains' applicability criteria. This result in confusion, making it difficult for supply chain professionals to understand concepts in order to correctly select and align the adequate supply chain model to their own business reality.

In addition to the confusion about the terminology, these approaches have been inconclusive because they don't have evolved from the concepts and general theories to methods oriented toward facilitate its application in business. The contribution of the Supply Chain Roadmap is to move from general theory to an applied method through the development of an organized and systematic method oriented to understand evaluate and reformulate supply chain strategy in alignment with business strategy.

Chapter 02
Supply Chain Roadmap

A new glance about supply chain strategy

Theory behind Supply Chain Roadmap method

Three Perspectives for Formulating Supply Chain Strategy

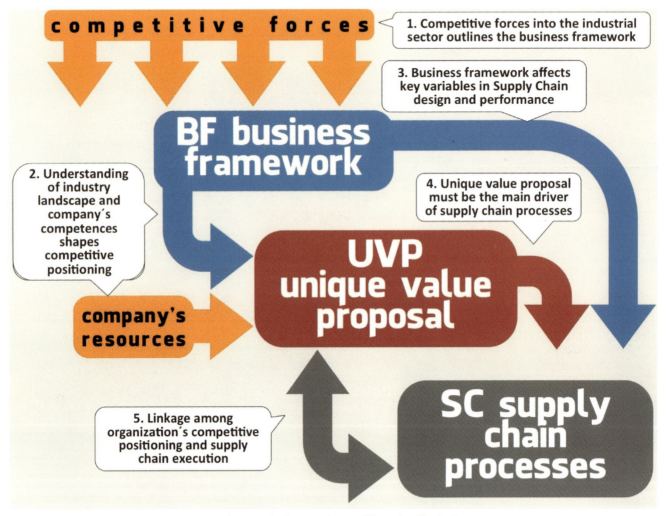

Figure 2.1 Perspectives of Supply Chain Strategy

An organization's supply chain strategy is shaped by the interrelation among three main perspectives (see Figure 2.1)[xiii]:
- The industry and target market landscape, called "Business Framework,"
- The organization's competitive positioning, expressed as the "Unique Value Proposal," and
- The internal perspective of the supply chain activities, termed "Supply Chain Processes"

Business Framework

Competitive forces (e.g., competitors, suppliers, customers, and substitute products, as were defined by Michael Porter in 1980s) in the industrial sector outline the Business Framework (BF), which is the landscape of the industry sector in which the organization competes focused into the target market. A proper definition of the Business Framework allows an understanding of the behaviors, economical aspects, and supply–demand balance as viewed by customers and suppliers, and the comprehension of the state of the technology and its impact on the economical aspects of the business.

Business Framework is comprised of three dimensions of the external forces affecting competition into the industry:

- **Sourcing View**, which describes the industry's suppliers in order to understand sourcing complexity and the economical aspects of the sourcing, and their effects on the competition in the industry.
- **Technology View**, which is defined as the understanding of the technological and economical factors related to the transformation processes—manufacturing, assembly, and/or conversion processes, or, in a most general way, processes oriented to "make" the product—and their effects on the forces of competition.
- **Demand View**, which is the understanding of customer behaviors and the economical aspects of the demand of the target market, and their effect on the competition at the industry.

Unique Value Proposal

Business Framework, in conjunction with the resources and competences of the company, constitutes the main driver for defining the Unique Value Proposal (UVP), which defines the competitive positioning of the company in terms of the attributes of the product and of the services associated with the product. The UVP marks the intersection between the understanding of the market's needs and the organization's competencies. With that, it is necessary to understand which of the market's needs can be satisfied in a differentiated manner, supported by the company's current competencies, or which competencies must be developed in order to satisfy the market's needs, which until now have not been exploited by the competition.

A recommended approach for defining the attributes of the UVP are the concepts of "Order Qualifiers" and "Order Winners," described in 1995 by Terry Hill, a leading figure in the field of operations management and Emeritus Fellow at the University of Oxford. These concepts define, respectively, the minimum requirements for being considered as a relevant option by customers and the performance aspects that best differentiate the company from its competitors and therefore help to win customer orders. The company must define which attributes are irrelevant to its competitive positioning, which attributes must be developed at a level similar to that of the industry (Order Qualifiers) in order to be considered as a relevant option by the customer, and which attributes should be developed at the highest level of performance and experience so as to differentiate itself from its competitors (Order Winners).

The UVP perspective incorporates two dimensions of the company's competitive positioning:

- **Product attributes**, which are the main attributes of the company's value proposal in terms of product and consider how these attributes are compared against relevant competitors.
- **Service attributes**, which are the main attributes of the company's value proposal in terms of the services that complement the product and consider how these attributes are compared against relevant competitors.

Figure 2.2 shows the stages of understanding and formulation of a company's Unique Value Proposal. The key aspect of the formulation of the UVP is to understand and reformulate company's offer compared against offers of relevant competitors at the industry:

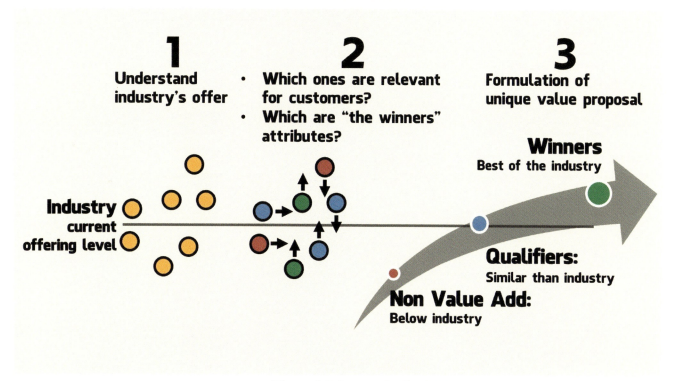

Figure 2.2 Steps to Define UVP

First, attributes offered by the company and/or relevant competitors in the industry should be identified, which are represented in yellow color.

Second, attributes offered by the company are compared with the level of offering of the relevant competitors at the industry, and is defined which should be the proper level of offering of each attribute:

- Which of the current attributes offered by the company may be **reduced or eliminated** from the company's Unique Value Proposal because they do not add value? These attributes are represented by red dots.

- Which attributes should be **maintained in a similar level** to the relevant competitors in the industry? These attributes are represented by blue dots.
- Which attributes could be **enhanced in comparison to the relevant competitors** in the industry, in order to offer a significant difference in the customer's perception? These are represented by green dots.

Third, based on above, the attributes are categorized according to the offering level in comparison with the relevant competitors at the industry, and the reformulated company's Unique Value Proposal is obtained.

Product and service attributes compose the UVP, which is an important component of the business strategy. It is not, however, the entire business strategy, because this involves other important components out of the scope of the supply chain strategy, as shown in Figure 2.3.

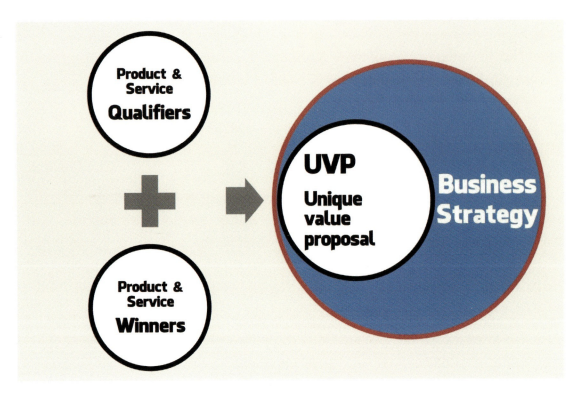

Figure 2.3 UVP in Business Strategy

Supply Chain Processes

Supply Chain Processes comprise the end-to-end activities necessary to plan and fulfill the customer's orders, starting from the sourcing of materials and components, passing though the transformation processes, and ending into the delivery of product to the customers.

Supply Chain Processes must be aligned to the company's strategy, and not the other way. Consequently, Supply Chain Processes should be designed for assuring the accomplishment of the offering level of the company's Unique Value Proposal.

Supply Chain Processes are defined by four dimensions, which define the connection among supply chain activities:

- **Sourcing**, which includes the main factors governing connection of supply chain activities with the supplier's supply chain.
- **Plan & Make**, which details the proper connection and combination within the supply chain activities: source, make, and delivery.
- **Demand fulfillment**, which is the tactical factor governing connection of supply chain activities with the customer's supply chain.
- **Managerial Focus**, which represents the linkage and alignment between an organization's competitive positioning and its Supply Chain Processes. The connection between these two areas is governed by the decision-making process and is driven by the supply chain's managerial focus.

Supply Chain Processes are governed by several factors (see Figure 2.4), and they will be reviewed in detail in the next section.

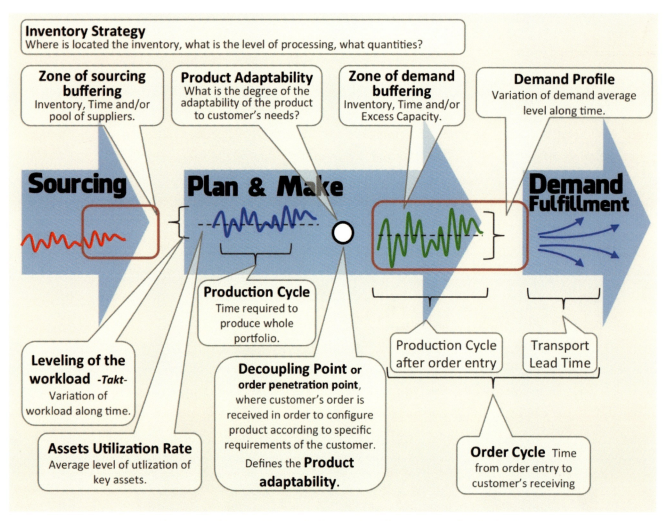

Figure 2.4 Interaction and Connection Among Supply Chain Factors

The Map

As was explained above the three perspectives, Business Framework, Unique Value Proposal and Supply Chain Processes, are comprised of nine dimensions, which are outlined in the map of the supply chain strategy (see Figure 2.5). This constitutes the core elements of the Supply Chain Roadmap method, providing an organized and systematic method to formulate supply chain strategy in alignment with business strategy.

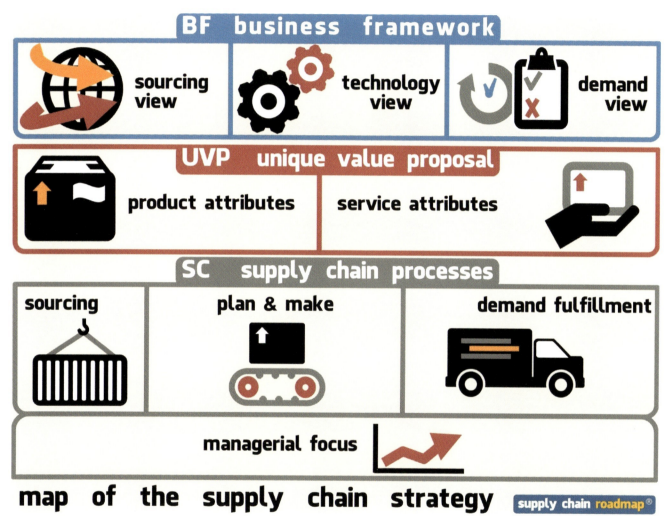

Figure 2.5 Map of the Supply Chain Strategy

SECTION 2: Tools of the Supply Chain Roadmap

The Supply Chain Roadmap provides a method designed to gather information about the business environment, the organization's competitive positioning, and its current supply chain profile in order to characterize a supply chain strategy under a single drawing called "The Map." The map constitutes in the main tool of the method.

The evaluation of the properness of this strategy uses other three tools: Common Patterns, Archetypes, and Feasibility Matrix. The four tools will be described in Chapters 3 to 6.

Chapter 03
The Map

A diagrammatic representation of the supply chain strategy.

Tool 1: The Map

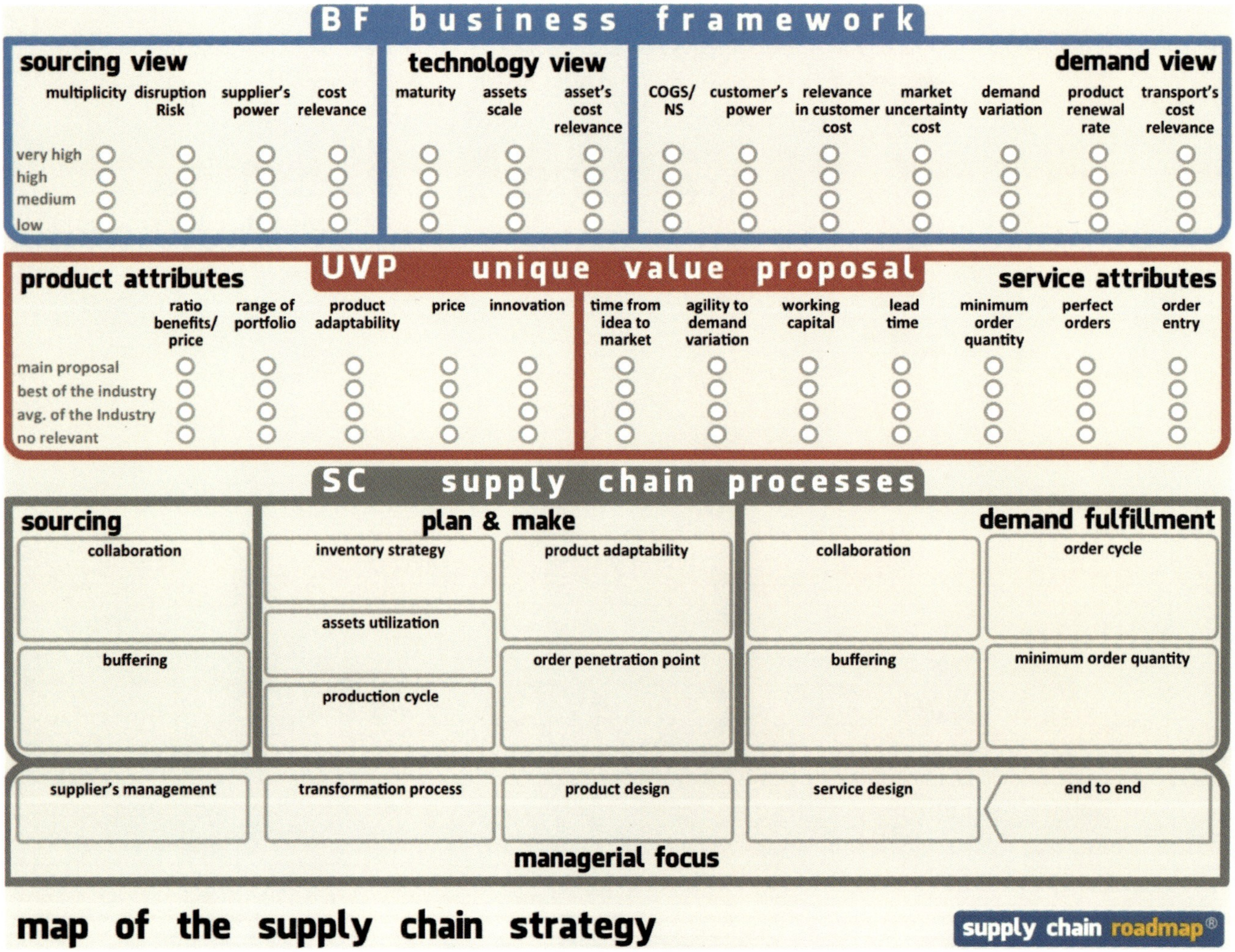

Figure 3.1 The Map

The Map is the graphic representation of the organization's supply chain strategy under three perspectives: Business Framework, Unique Value Proposal, and Supply Chain Processes. It allows visualization and understanding of the three perspectives on a single page.

A printable version of the map is available on www.SupplyChainRoadmap.com.

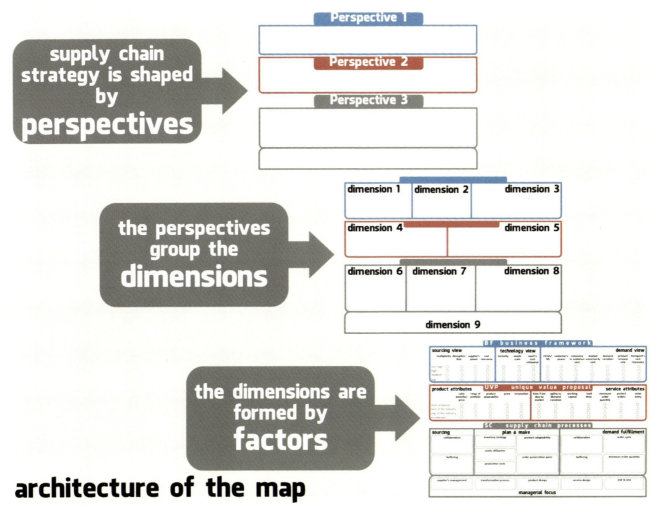

Figure 3.2 Architecture of the Map

The Map describes the three perspectives (Business Framework, Unique Value Proposal, and Supply Chain Processes), nine dimensions (Sourcing View, Technology View, Demand View, product attributes, service attributes, sourcing, plan & make, demand fulfillment, and managerial focus), and forty-two factors of the supply chain strategy, as shown in Figures 3.1 and 3.2.

The Map is used in two different ways:
- **Assessment of an organization's supply chain.** This describes the supply chain in two different stages: the current situation and the desired future situation.
- **Deployment of supply chain strategy.** This describes the supply chain strategy of an organization as a tool for training and aligning people around a unique strategy.

Business Framework Perspective

As was mentioned previously, the Business Framework is composed of three dimensions: Sourcing, Technology, and Demand. Understanding the industry landscape of each view should be realized under the common and general perspective of all the relevant competitors competing into the market. Organizations must avoid interpretations that apply only for the company under assessment, and the Business Framework should be used only in interpretations that apply for all the relevant players in the market.

Sourcing View

As was explained in chapter 2, Sourcing View describes the industry's suppliers in order to understand sourcing complexity and the economical aspects of the sourcing, as well as their effects on the competition in the industry. Sourcing View is comprised of four factors: Complexity, Disruption Risk, Supplier's Power, and Relevance of sourcing in total cost.

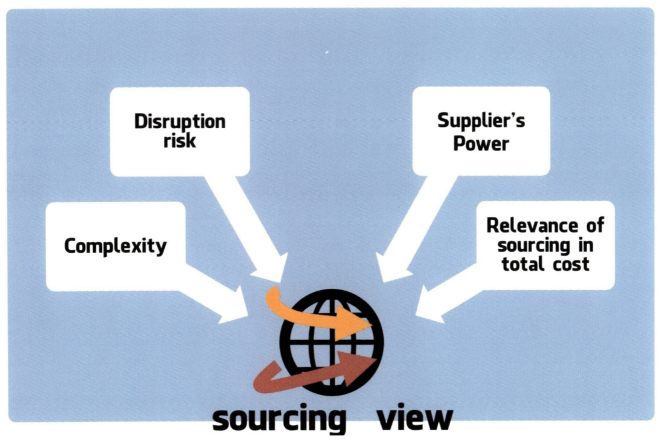

Figure 3.3 Factors of Sourcing View

Complexity refers to the understanding of the pluralism of suppliers and sourcing SKUs. This factor is highly relevant, because sourcing becomes more complex when number of SKUs, suppliers, and/or length of lead-time makes greater. Complexity is qualified in four levels:

a) Low: In a supply chain with a low number of sourcing SKUs sourced by a small number of suppliers, most suppliers have short lead-time. Typically, these are domestic vendors.

b) Medium: one of the three sourcing variables (sourced SKUs, number of suppliers, or sourcing lead-time) becomes greater and creates a relevant complexity for the management.

c) High: two of the three sourcing variables (sourced SKUs, number of suppliers or sourcing lead-time) becomes greater and creates a relevant complexity for the management.

d) Very High: A supply chain with a high number of sourcing SKUs sourced by a high number of suppliers in which most suppliers have a long lead-time. Typically, these are overseas vendors and/or long a complex production processes.

Disruption Risk refers to the risk of total or partial disruption of sourcing of materials or components required for the production of the products offered by the company to their customers. Disruption risk is qualified in four levels:

a) Low: At this level, there is negligible risk of supply interruption by high reliability of suppliers.

b) Medium: At this level, several alternatives to substitution (i.e., other suppliers and/or other materials or components) can be promptly activated without affecting the continuity of the operation.

c) High: At this level, there are some alternatives of substitution, which can be activated in a short or medium length horizon, generally hours or a few days. Continuity of the operation, however, is affected by a few days.

d) Very High: At this level, it is likely that demand exceeds supply. There is an oligopoly and no replacement alternatives. When there is collusion among the members of the oligopoly, they could prioritize those customers who pay a better price, creating a price escalation and reducing sourcing to those customers whose opposed to pay a higher price. In the case of disruption, continuity of the operation could be affected severely, passing from some days to several weeks.

Supplier's Power refers to the balance of power in the relationship among suppliers and customers (the industry). It is qualified in a scale of four levels:

a) Low: Relationship among suppliers and industry is dominated by these last. At this level, it is likely that supply exceeds demand, and there may be multiple alternatives of sourcing or multiple alternatives of substitute materials or components.

b) Medium: At this level, there exists a market with a balance between demand and supply. There is a high level of entry barriers to global suppliers. However, when global prices reduce in a level that matches domestic prices, the alternatives of sourcing (global vendors) increase and the relationship of power becomes unbalanced and moves, increasing the power of the industry.

c) High: At this level, there is a balanced market demand and supply, but high entry barriers reduce alternatives of new suppliers for the industry (import or newer domestic players) because suppliers hold all the power.

d) Very High: At this level, there is likely limited competition and the supply is shorter than demand requirements, and consequence of that suppliers dominate the market.

Sourcing's Cost Relevance refers to the magnitude of significance of the cost of sourced materials and/or components compared to the total cost of the finished product.

a) Low: At this level, the cost of external supplies is very low compared to the total cost structure of the product (<25% cost of goods sold [COGS]).

b) Medium: Most of COGS is associated with the transformation processes, rather than with components or external supply.

c) High: The cost added by the transformation process and supplies costs are of similar magnitude within the COGS.

d) Very High: Cost aggregated by the transformation process is low compared with the cost of supplies (> 75% COGS)

Technology View

As was explained in Chapter 2, Technology View is defined as the understanding of the technological and economical factors related to the transformation processes—manufacturing, assembly, and/or conversion processes, or, in a most general way, processes oriented to make the product—and their effects on the forces of competition. Technology View is comprised of three factors: maturity of technology of transformation processes, scale of productive assets, and relevance of assets in total cost of product.

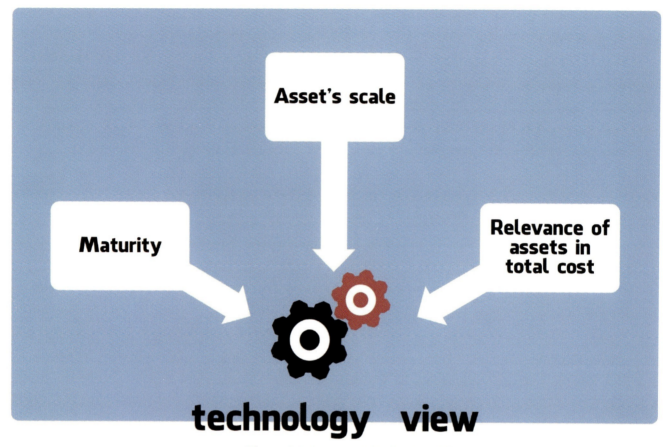

Figure 3.4 Factors of Technology View

Maturity refers to the understanding of the stage of development of the technology associated with the transformation processes and raw materials and components:

a) Low: At this level, technology is in an introductory stage (near state of art) where the product life cycle is very short due to the continuous changes in the technology.

b) Medium: At this level, technology in a continuous development and has already surpassed the technical and economical difficulties associated with the initial stages of the technology life cycle.

c) High: At this level, technology undergoes some sporadic changes, which can generate minor differentiations in the production processes among manufactures for short periods of time.

d) Very High: At this level, technology is mature and affordable for many players in the market, and differentiation among competitors are associated with brand power, fashion trends, packaging, service attributes and/or secondary attributes.

Scale of Productive Assets relates to the magnitude of increased of capacity of production when current or new players into the industry introduce new assets—*machines and/or production lines*—.

a) Low: At this level, productive assets are available at a very low capacity and industry is highly fragmented because the entry of a new competitor and/or expansion of capacity is not relevant in the balance of supply and demand.

b) Medium: At this level, the entry of new players into the market and/or the expansion of productive assets of existing competitors has low relevance (<5%) in the balance of supply and demand.

c) High: At this level, entry of new competitors into the market and/or expansion of productive assets of existing ones, has significant relevance (5 to 10%) in the balance of supply and demand.

d) Very High: At this level, the entry of new productive assets at the industry has significant importance (>10 to 15%) in the balance of supply and demand.

Relevance of Assets in Total Cost relates to the magnitude of the fixed cost of the assets in relation to the total cost of the product. This is one of the most significant factors affecting the design of the supply chain strategy.

a) Low: At this level, cost of assets is almost negligible in the cost structure. Rate of assets utilization likely is not relevant to the bottom line of the company.

b) Medium: When the rate of utilization of the assets drops significantly (30 to 40%), it will significantly affect company's financial results.

c) High: When the rate of utilization of assets falls in medium levels (10 to 30% of the average), the financial performance of the company is likely strongly affected.

d) Very High: When the rate of utilization of assets falls at low levels (5 to 10% of the average), the financial performance of the company is likely strongly affected.

Demand View

As was explained in chapter 2, Demand View is the understanding of customer behaviors and the economical aspects of the demand of the target market, and their effect on the competition at the industry. Demand View is composed of five factors: relevance of the product's cost in the customer's cost structure, market uncertainty cost, relevance of transport cost, customer's power, and demand variation.

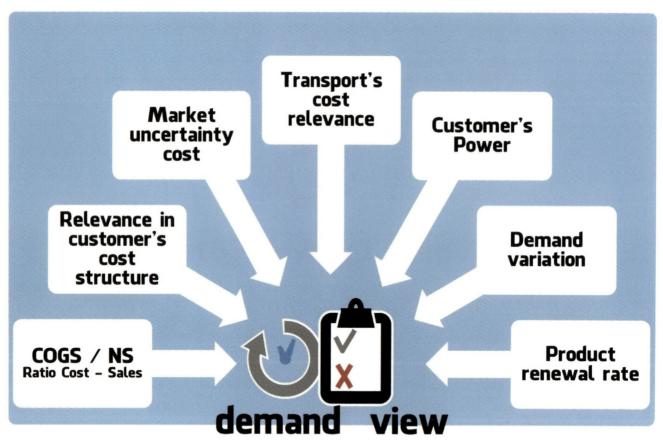

Figure 3.5 Factors of Demand View

Ratio Cost/Sales (COGS/NS) defines the relationship between product cost and product price. It is a key measure of the size of typical gross margins in the industry.

a) Low: It is a category of high-gross margin products in which the biggest expenses are associated with sales, distribution, and/or management.

b) Medium: It is a category with significantly high gross margins (> 30 to 40%).

c) High: It is a category of products with gross margins between 20 and 30%.

d) Very High: It is a category with a very low gross margin (<20%).

Relevance in Customer's Cost Structure defines the relative importance in terms of cost of the product or of the product's category under analysis in the cost structure of the customers.

a) Low: The cost of the product is not significant in the cost structure of the customer. The customer is likely to make long-term business, and sporadically, customers conduct a market comparative review in order to verify competitiveness of current supplier.

b) Medium: The cost of the product or category of products is a significant cost in the cost structure of the customer, but the product or category of products is not in its focus permanently. The customer may evaluate prices of the market once or twice a year.

c) High: The cost of the product or category of products is a significant component in the cost structure of the customer, and the customer maintains a strict and permanent review of the market price.

d) Very High: The cost of the product or category of products is probably the most important or one of the most important components in the client's cost structure. The customer maintains a permanent and strict review of the price in the domestic and global market.

Market Uncertainty Cost refers to the costs associated to the unbalance of demand and supply, which is composed of the sum of markdown of products for compensating excess of supply and profit of lost sales when demand exceeds supply. These costs, which reflect the unstable and fragile balance between lost sales and product obsolescence, arise as a result of the consequences of the degree of demand predictability.

a) Low: When demand is highly predictable, and as a result, there is not presence of breakdown of stock, price reduction, or inventory write-off.

b) **Medium:** Uncertainty of demand is present and as consequence of that, sometimes successful products are out of stock, and unsuccessful products are affected by price reduction (about 20%) to ensure inventory depletion.

c) **High:** It is very common that successful products are out of stock and unsuccessful products are affected by price reduction (about 20%) to ensure inventory depletion.

d) **Very High:** It is very common that successful products sell out quickly and unsuccessful products require significant price reduction (more than 30 to 40%) and perhaps even inventory write off.

Transport's Cost Relevance relates to the relative importance of the cost of transportation in the total cost of the product, which is governed by the relationship product price/product cube, *-the amount of space, measured in cubic units, that the product occupies-*.

a) **Low:** The relationship product price/product cube is very high, which makes the cost of transport is practically negligible in the cost structure.

b) **Medium:** The cost of transport is a relevant factor in the cost structure; however, it is not highly significant (< 2 to 3% of Net Sales [NS])

c) **High:** The cost of transport is significant in the cost structure of the product (3 to 10% NS).

d) **Very High:** The relationship price/product cube is low because the cost of transportation is highly significant, reaching double digits (> 10% NS) in the cost structure. Probably is a "must" to dispatch in full truckload in order to increase the truck filling efficiency and therefore optimize transportation cost.

Customer's Power refers to the balance of power in the relationship among industry and customers. It is qualified in a scale of four levels:

a) **Low:** The market is dominated by the industry, probably demand exceeds supply and/or there are few alternatives of sourcing and/or there are not alternatives of substitute materials/components.

b) **Medium:** There is a balance between demand/supply, and entry barriers are high, reducing the entry of new alternative players into the industry (import or domestic).

c) **High:** There is a balance between demand/supply, but changes in global prices can increase the supply of foreign producers, giving customers more choices.

d) Very High: the clients dominate the market, probably supply exceeds demand and/or multiple alternatives of sourcing exist and/or substitute products.

Demand Variation defines the magnitude of the changes of the demand profile, i.e., quantity and size of the customer orders over the time, answering the question "How smooth or shifting is the demand?"

a) Low: The demand profile has short and smooth variations, as in the demand for perishable products such as dairy or bread.

b) Medium: The demand profile has low and medium size peaks (around 20 to 30% of the average demand), as in the demand for consumer goods as personal care products or home care products.

c) High: The demand profile has high size peaks (around 50% of the average demand), as in the demand for fashion products (e.g., products associated to trends or to characters of seasonal movies.

d) Very High: Occasional and unpredictable demands of very high magnitude. Typical of the demand for services or products associated with unexpected events such as repairs, projects, or emergencies.

Product Renewal Rate refers to the rate of introduction of new SKUs with medium to major changes into the category.

a) Low: Stable products, which, with minor changes (e.g., packaging, minor benefits,) remain on the market for long periods of time. For example some fast-moving consumer goods such as shampoo, toilet paper, everyday use alkaline batteries, packaged sugar, etc.

b) Medium: Products are renewed in an annual basis, affected by fashion and/or changes in technology (e.g., clothing, cell phones, computers).

c) High: The products are continually renewed (weeks/months) to be consistent with latest fashion and media trends (e.g., fashion clothing, film-related products).

d) Very High: Companies whose products are manufactured to unique specifications for each order; generally customers are not recurrent and/or there are long periods of time between orders.

Unique Value Proposal Perspective

As explained, the UVP is the result of the understanding of the market's needs and the organization's competencies. In essence the UVP should state the company's competitive strategy in terms of product and service attributes. In order to create a differentiated positioning in the market, it is necessary to use one of the following approaches:
- Understand which of the market's needs can be satisfied in a differentiated manner, supported by the company's current competencies,
- Which competencies must be developed in order to create new attributes, which until now have not been exploited by the competition,
- A combination of both.

Product and service attributes should be qualified in a comparative view against relevant competitors in the target market. This comparison should be done with the customer's perception in mind. A reasonable way to understand comparative performance of an attribute against competitors is by a consumer panel or by a contest with customers, or other customer-centric feedback.

The attributes are qualified in a comparative scale of four levels:
- **Not relevant:** when an attribute is not present in the company's UVP or is performing below industry average under customer's perception.
- **Average of the industry:** when the attribute performs at a similar level than industry average. Typically, this is defined as an "Order Qualifier," which is an attribute that is required in order to be considered as an option of purchase by consumers and which provides the opportunity to compete against relevant competitors.
- **Best of the industry:** when the attribute performs at a level higher than industry average. Typically, this is defined as an "Order Winner," which is an attribute that could be the difference against competitors in order to be selected by the consumers.
- **Main proposal:** when the attribute is not only the best of the industry, but is the main valuable attribute of the UVP of the company.

Product Attributes

Qualification of the product performance under customer's perception is realized under five attributes: ratio benefits/price, range of portfolio, product adaptability, product price, and product innovation.

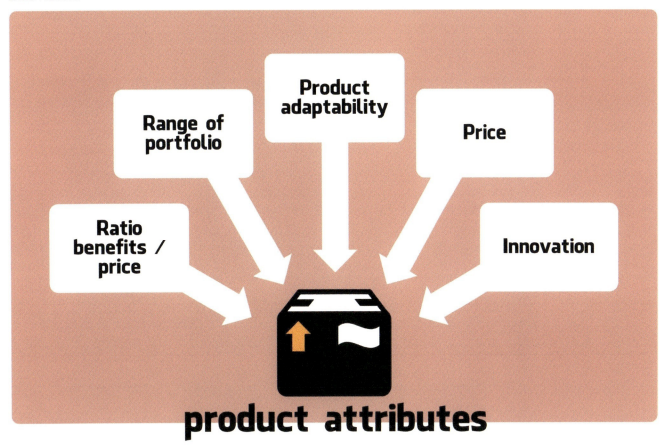

Figure 3.6 Product Attributes

Ratio benefits/price: A ratio that examines the benefits of the product versus price compared to relevant competitors in the target market

Range of portfolio: How broad the company's product portfolio is compared to relevant competitors in the target market

Product adaptability: A comparison of the power of proposed product adaptability when compared to relevant competitors. Product adaptability is determined by the attributes of the product that could be personalized according to each customer's needs.

Price: A comparison of the price of the product with respect to relevant competitors in the target market

Innovation: A measure of the level of uniqueness of yours products, it means that products have unique and exclusive benefits that are obvious to customers when compared with products of relevant competitors into the target market

Service Attributes

Qualification of the service performance under customer's perception is realized under seven attributes: time from idea to market, agility to demand variation, lowest level of working capital, lead-time from order to receiving, minimum order quantity, perfect orders, and order entry process.

Time from idea to market weighs how long it takes for an organization to move from idea to introducing new products and innovations to the market.

Agility to demand variations considers the organization's ability to meet unexpected and expedited orders, either in quantity above regular demand and/or a delivery time below regular lead-time.

Working capital examines the capacity of the company to offer its customers a continuous replenishment of product in order to reduce inventory level at customer's facility and, consequently, reduce the customer's working capital.

Lead-time considers how long it takes from the moment a customer places the order to the moment a customer receives the product.

Minimum order quantity looks at whether the organization has a minimum order policy in terms of transport load (i.e., total order value and/or minimum volume of the product) and/or manufacturing batch (SKU order size).

Perfect Orders is defined as the percentage of orders delivered on time, complete on quantity, and without errors on the delivery, including cases wrong labeled, defective products, or erroneous invoicing, among others.

Order entry examines how friendly, accurate, and fast the process of order entry from the customer's perspective is. This is a qualitative measure, which could be associated with the level of satisfaction of the customer experience when ordering a product from the company.

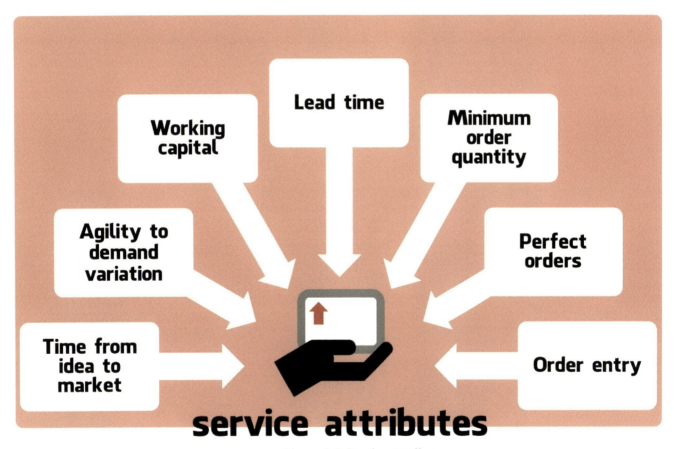

Figure 3.7 Service Attributes

Supply Chain Processes Perspective

As explained in Chapter 2, Supply Chain Processes comprise the end-to-end activities necessary to plan and fulfill customer orders, starting from the sourcing of materials and components, passing though the transformation processes, and ending into the delivery of product to the customers.

The Supply Chain Processes perspective is comprised of sixteen factors, which shape the connection among the supply chain activities, giving structure to the organization's supply chain strategy. Each factor has several patterns, and for each factor, the proper pattern in the organization under analysis should be identified in order to create its map of supply chain strategy.

Sourcing Process

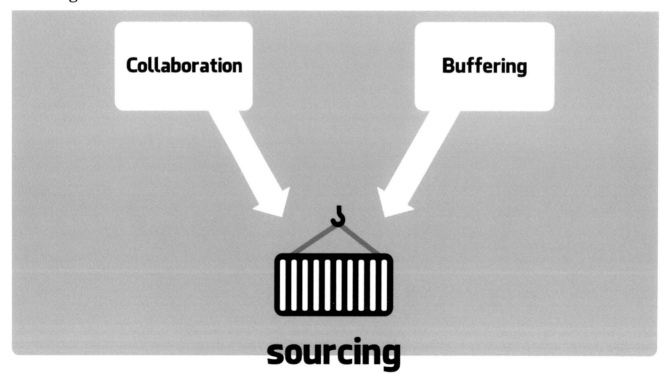

Figure 3.8 Factors of sourcing process.

Sourcing process is highly relevant for the supply chain strategy, especially in industries facing a dominant position of the suppliers, or inclusive, in markets with supply shortage and/or high risk of sourcing disruption.

Sourcing process includes the main factors governing connection of supply chain activities of the company with supplier's supply chain, and it is characterized by two factors: collaboration with customers and buffering of sourcing variation.

Collaboration, in essence, it is to cooperate and share information with the suppliers, aiming for creating, synergies with them, and anticipating changes on the sourcing that could affect the organization's supply chain.. There are six typical patterns of collaboration with suppliers:

a) Understanding the supplier's "available to promise" at any time. "Available to promise" is the vendor's ability to commit deliveries to customers. A collaborative relationship oriented to understand supplier's available to promise allows to the customer—and the industry—to have greater certainty before the organization commits to delivering a product or service to its own customers, reducing risk of noncompliance and poor service.

b) Cooperation with some key suppliers, reporting long-term capacity needs. Cooperation is useful for planning supplier's assets capacity in the long term. This pattern is recommended when sourcing capacity is constrained and supplier's expansion of capacity is a long process, giving visibility to the suppliers about the future requirements of the industry in order to avoid a shortage of capacity.

c) Cooperation with key suppliers to anticipate aggregate demand at family level. In some scenarios, cooperation is required to anticipate future demand in order to book supplier's capacity for the short and medium term. For the purpose of avoiding the complexity of calculating the forecast at SKU level, the forecast is prepared at level of semi-finished products and/or grouped by family of SKUs with similar characteristics, allowing to calculate and book the capacity requirements.

d) Cooperation to anticipate market trends and/or joint design. According to market trends, the joint effort with key suppliers to develop materials and/or components, focused in terms of fashion and technological development. This approach is useful when an organization's portfolio is highly changeable, in order to reduce time for adopting most recent tendencies in materials or components.

e) Not relevant. Collaboration is not present, either because the company does not pay enough attention to the creation of synergies with suppliers, or because the company handles an opportunistic approach, avoiding close relationships, and the organization takes advantage of changing markets and related trends.

f) Strategic relationships with key suppliers to create synergies. A closer relationship aimed at eliminating non value-added functions, or redundant functions, which thereby optimizes service and inventory costs on both sides (manufacturer–supplier).

Buffering defines the method used for compensating sourcing variations, in order to avoid disruption of the supply chain. There are five characteristics patterns of buffering:

a) Pool of suppliers for critical resources. If demand is uncertain, it is necessary to maintain a pool of suppliers with whom your organization could share materials and/or resources as dictated by the specific needs at any time.

b) Inventory + pool of suppliers. Sourcing uncertainty is high, thus a mixed buffering is required in order to ensure sourcing availability and business continuity on scenarios of sourcing shortage. On one side, inventory is kept at intentionally high levels in the organization, and on the other, a pool of suppliers is shared for each material or component in order to ensure multiple sources of sourcing.

c) Inventory + a strategic supplier for each key component. In this approach, the organization seeks collaborative long-term synergies and long-term agreements with a single supplier for each key component.

d) Inventory + best cost supplier at each time. When materials and components are available at similar specifications from several sources, the organization can employ an opportunistic approach to buffering, maintain a high inventory, and find the best cost provider each time.

e) Pool of suppliers. In this approach, there is a pool of suppliers for each key material or component in order to ensure availability. If a single vendor is not sufficient for crucial materials and components, it is necessary to work with a group of providers in order to ensure multiple sources of sourcing, and therefore product availability. Inventory is maintained at low levels because the availability of the product in the market is very high.

Plan and Make Processes

Plan & Make includes the main factors governing the transformation processes, ensuring the proper synchronization among five factors: inventory, production cycle, product adaptability, order penetration point, and assets utilization. An unsuitable synchronization among them unbalances the ratio among inventory and productivity, generating poor service or financial underperformance.

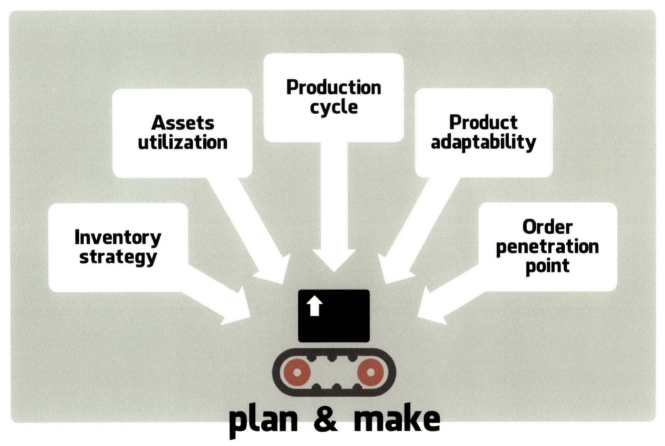

Figure 3.9 Factors of plan & make processes.

Inventory Strategy describes an approach to define the proper placement of the inventory into the supply chain and the relationship between inventory and efficiency.

In order to define the proper selection of the pattern used for this factor it is important to answer these questions:
- Where is located the major part of the inventory?
- What is the degree of processing of the inventory?
- How is the relationship between the inventory level and production efficiency?

There are six typical patterns for inventory strategy:

a) A single batch per SKU, according to forecast of the collection. In this pattern, inventory is fully processed before receiving customer order. Inventory is located at the end of the supply chain as finished product. Products are in continuous renewal, and so they are produced in a unique and single batch, limiting availability in the market to the produced batch units. The product will not be produced again, in order to provide exclusivity and feeling of scarcity, which encourage impulse buying.

b) High level of inventory to optimize production efficiency. Inventory is fully processed before receiving customer order; inventory is located at the end of supply chain as finished product, but contrary to the previous pattern, the products will again be produced in order to maintain permanent availability of the product at the market. Production efficiency is a key driver of the supply chain, and so inventory level could be high in order to increase the batch size and reduce production frequency, and, consequently, optimize productivity.

c) Small and frequent batches to increase inventory turns. Inventory is fully processed before receiving customer order; inventory is located at the end of supply chain as finished product and, similar to the previous pattern, the products will again be produced in order to maintain permanent availability of the product at the market. As inventory turns is a key driver of the supply chain, production batches are small and more frequent, which reduces productivity but increases inventory turns.

d) Low inventory level & inventory pooling. Inventory is in raw materials/components or semi-finished product before receiving customer order. In this approach, an organization pools inventory with suppliers and/or competitors in order to increase available to promise at any moment.

e) Materials/components under a common platform. Inventory is in raw materials or purchased components before receiving customer order. Because product specifications are unique for each customer, the company doesn't hold finished product; consequently, minimum order quantities should be equal to minimum economic production batches.

f) Inventory just before product divergence point (PDP). PDP is the activity in the supply chain where the product takes features that are exclusive for a customer or group of customers and makes the product is not suitable for sale to other customers. Inventory is in components or semi-finished product located before PDP. Processes before PDP are driven by productivity, and so inventory could be high. PDP and downstream processes are driven by zero inventory; thus, the organization produces finished product only when a customer order is received in order to meet customer's requirements; consequently, productivity is negatively affected.

Assets utilization rate describes the level of utilization of main assets, understood as the ratio between scheduled hours and total hours—24 hours, 7 days a week. There are five typical patterns for assets utilization rate:

a) Low-Medium. Utilization is below 40 to 50% of installed capacity, and in some cases installed capacity could be on stand-by and/or for occasional use. In this pattern, it is likely that the organization operates one shift per day and that there is available capacity in this shift and/or that equipment is available to deal with times of peak demand.

b) Medium. Utilization is around 60 to 70% of installed capacity. In this pattern, the organization may operate two shifts per day and/or three shifts in order to have enough agility for peak demands.

c) High before PDP, medium in PDP and after. Utilization rate before PDP is around 85 to 90% of installed capacity. In this pattern, the organization operates around the clock with only minor stoppages (e.g., one to four days per month). In PDP and downstream processes, the company may operate two shifts per day and/or three shifts in order to have enough agility for peak demands.

d) High-Very High. Utilization rate is around 85 to 90% of installed capacity. 24 hours per day, there are some minor scheduled stoppages (one to four days by month).

e) Very High. Utilization rate is higher than 90% of installed capacity. In this pattern, the organization operates 24 hours per day and 365 days a year and scheduled stoppages are scarce (one to four days by year).

Production cycle describes the criteria used to define the length of time used for producing the whole product portfolio.

In order to define the proper selection of the pattern used for this factor is relevant to answer these questions:

- What is the main criterion used for defining the production cycle?
- How are the relationships among production cycle, inventory level, and production efficiency?

Patterns for production cycle:

a) As short as possible to reduce batch size. Company is oriented to produce small and frequent batches for each SKU in order to ensure high inventory turns.

b) As long as possible to increase batch size and efficiency. Company is oriented to ensure high efficiency rates, and so batch sizes are high and the production cycle is long.

c) As short as possible to reduce time from idea to market. Company is oriented to renew its product portfolio in a continuous way, introducing SKUs with short lifetime in the market, in order to offer a constantly updated portfolio. Consequently, production is oriented to one time and small batches of each SKU, and the production cycle is short.

d) Long before PDP, short in PDP and downstream. Production before PDP is oriented to ensure high efficiency rates, and so the production cycle is long. Production in PDP and subsequent processes are oriented to small batches—probably one batch per customer order—and so the production cycle is short.

e) Variable according to customer orders accepted in queue. Production is scheduled according to customer orders accepted, and so the production cycle is variable for each order, according to the ratio between orders in queue and available capacity.

f) As short as possible to reduce lead-time. Company's portfolio is infinite, meaning orders are fulfilled according to the specific needs of each customer but that very few orders are produced at the same moment and that there is a very high level of excess capacity. As a result, the production cycle is very short.

Product adaptability describes the extent of product customization offered to customers, and it is determined by the attributes that are allowed to be adapted according to the needs of customers. This is an important factor because it defines the order penetration point, which governs inventory strategy and assets utilization.

There are six levels of product customization:

a) Standardized product. Regardless of the extent of the company's portfolio, each portfolio product is manufactured under a single common specification for all customers. Most consumer products fall under this category.

b) Continuous portfolio renewal. All products in the portfolio are standardized, and most of these products have a short life cycle, so SKUs are only manufactured one time—in single and unique production batches—so that the portfolio of products are kept in continuous renewal. Most fast fashion products (e.g., products associated with themes and/or characters such as movies, sports, events) fall within this category.

c) Configurable product. This pattern takes advantage of an important concept PDP, the point of the production processes when the product takes unique specifications for a specific customer or group of customers. This concept is applied in two cases and/or the combination of them.

In the first case, products are formed from the assembly of various components or parts, some of which have multiple options of specifications. The selection of specifications of the components that have multiple options is made by the customer when placing the order, such as in computer assembly in which customers have multiple choices for the configuration of processors, memory, cards, etc.

In the second case, products are partially processed (e.g., semi-finished product) under common specifications applicable to all customers, and, pending processing, are made after receiving customer order when the unique specifications from each customer are known. This case is called postponement because common processes are made before receiving customer orders and because pending processes are postponed until receiving customer orders, as in the manufacture of corrugated boxes in which a group of products for multiple customers share the same corrugated cardboard but the dimensions and printing of each type of box is different for each SKU.

d) Customizable product. This refers to products for which the PDP is located at the beginning of the manufacturing processes. In some cases, raw materials or components may be unique to a customer or group of customers, such as in the manufacture of flavors and/or components for the food industry.

e) Adaptable processes. Adaptable processes are applied when it is required to design a unique, specific solution (consisting of the product itself, and the services provided with this) to each customer order. Usually customers are not recurring, and they seek a specific and quick solution to a problem or unforeseen situation. The design solution involves the design of the product and the design of the product manufacturing process, whereby the production process or manufacturing and/or transformation must be flexible and reconfigurable to meet the needs of each case. Adaptable processes are used, for example, when manufacturing parts to meet machine stoppages or for dressmakers, which meet the ability to reconfigure the layout and process flow for several types of garments with quick response.

Order Penetration Point (OPP), is the point of the supply chain where the customer order is received. It defines the quantity of processing required after the customer order is received and the way in which it is scheduled the production.

There are five OPPs, according to the level of product processing required after receiving customer's order:

a) Make to Stock (MTS). In this category, the product is totally processed before the customer order is received. Production is scheduled according to an optimal sequence of production (optimizing time of setup among SKUs). When the production sequence reaches a specific SKU, production quantity is defined to replenish inventory up to a level, sufficient to meet sales and variations until the next production of the same SKU.

b) Make to forecast (MTF). In this category, the product is fully processed before customer orders are received. Production is scheduled according to a forecast for the period of sale. There is flexibility to produce additional quantities at the end of the sales period. MTF can be useful when end-of-month syndrome is very high. End-of-month syndrome refers when the sales of the month are concentrated in a very short period of days at the end of month.

c) Make to Order (MTO). In this category, the product is fully processed after receiving the customer order, according to unique specifications for each customer.

d) Make to Forecast, in some occasions Make to Order. In this category, MTO is the norm, but for customers with long-term agreements, MTF is used in order to ensure availability for them.

e) Configured to Order (CTO). In this category, the product is partially finished and/or components are manufactured and unassembled before receiving customer orders, and it is necessary to undergo additional processes after receiving customer orders, according to the unique specifications of the customers.

f) Designed to Order (DTO). In this category, a solution is designed, processes are reconfigured, and products are processed after receiving customer orders.

Demand Fulfillment Process

Demand fulfillment includes the tactical factor governing connection of supply chain activities with the customer's supply chain, and is characterized by four factors: collaborative relationships with customers, buffering of demand variation, order cycle, and minimum order quantity.

A suitable connection with customers is source of two main benefits over the supply chain:
(1) Creates a higher perception of service by customer, increasing the potential of future sales.
(2) Reduces any bullwhip effect over the supply chain, decreasing demand variation on the end to end supply chain -*Bullwhip effect refers to the enlargement and oscillation of demand as they flow from demand end through the supply chain to the sourcing end, creating nonexistent demands-*

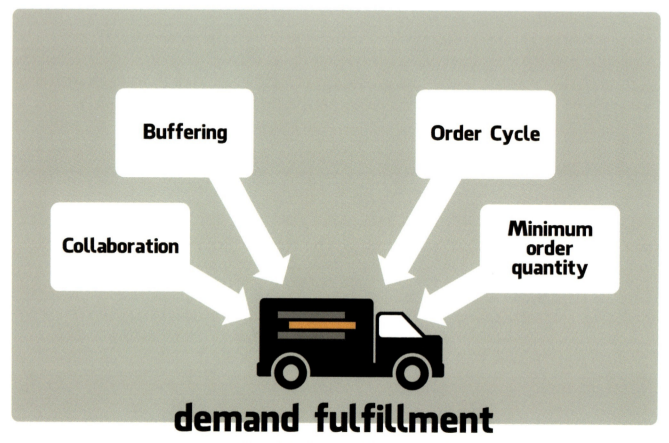

Figure 3.10 Factors of Demand Fulfillment

Collaboration. In essence, collaborative relationships define the way that a company shares information with their customers, creating synergies with them and anticipating changes on the demand that could affect the organization's supply chain. There are six typical patterns of collaboration with customers:

a) Strategic relationships with key customers to build synergies. A closer relationship aimed at eliminating non value-added functions, or redundant functions, which thereby optimizes service and inventory costs on both sides (industry–customer).

b) Not relevant. Collaboration is not present, either because the company does not pay enough attention to the creation of synergies with customers or because the customer prefers an opportunistic approach, avoiding close relationships, and takes advantage of changing markets and related trends.

c) Cooperation to anticipate market trends/joint design. Cooperation with key customers to understand market trends, focused in terms of fashion and technological development. This approach is useful when organization's portfolio is highly changeable, in order to reduce time for adopting most recent tendencies in ideas for new products.

d) Cooperation with key customers to anticipate aggregate demand at PDP. When companies produce under a postponement approach, they must anticipate demand requirements at PDP in order to book capacity in processes subsequent to PDP and anticipate production of semi-finished products and/or components.

e) Cooperation with some key customers to anticipate capacity requirements. Useful for long-term planning of assets capacity, this pattern is recommended when capacity is constrained and expansion of capacity is a long process, understanding future demand of the customers in order to avoid a shortage of capacity.

f) Understanding of available to promise at any moment. Collaboration is not relevant, but the industry provides customers with information about available to promise in order to facilitate an understanding of response capacity at the specific moment when customer orders are received.

Demand buffering defines the method used for compensating demand variations in order to avoid disruption of the customer's supply chain. Methods for compensating demand could be defined in terms of inventory, capacity, time, or a combination thereof. There are five characteristics patterns of buffering.

a) Stand by capacity + capacity pooling. Capacity is highly overdesigned in order to support unpredictable peaks of demand. In case of shortage, capacity of third parties is used to compensate shortage. Generally, the rate of utilization of assets is lower than 20% to 30% of installed capacity.

b) Extra capacity. Capacity is overdesigned in order to support peaks of demand. The rate of utilization of assets is generally around 60% to 80% of installed capacity.

c) Inventory before product decoupling point (PDP) + extra capacity after PDP. Company takes advantage of the postponement approach in order to process customer orders in a fast way; buffering is composed of inventory of both; (1) semi-finished products and/or components are located before PDP, and, (2) extra capacity in assets of PDP and subsequent processes.

d) Inventory of finished product. Enough inventory of fully finished product is available to buffer demand variations.

Order Cycle is the time between the order is placed and when the order is fulfilled.

a) Mainly Fixed cycle. This occurs when customer orders are received and dispatched in a fixed cycle. Generally, the product is finished before the customer order is received, such as when orders are received, say, every Tuesday and dispatched every Friday, or when orders are received the second day of the month and dispatched on day fifteen.

b) Mainly Fixed lead-time. Fixed lead-time refers to a fixed length of time from receiving a customer order until order delivery, independent of the moment when the customer order was received. Generally, the product is finished before the customer order is received, often within 24 hours.

c) Lead-time according to collection schedule. This applies when orders are dispatched at the beginning of a season. In some cases, additional replenishment is done in the middle of the season; in other cases there are no additional replenishments. Season length is specific to each business. For example, some multilevel marketing companies develop up to 18 seasons a year, while some trendy apparel companies develop 12 seasons a year. In this scheme, the collection schedule is driven by the ability to reduce the time from idea to market.

d) As short as possible according to orders in PDP queue. In this scheme, the product generally is partially finished before the customer order is received (a postponement approach), and it is necessary to undergo additional processes after receiving the customer order, according to the unique specifications of the customer. Order cycle is variable; it is specific for each situation, according to customer orders in queue at PDP.

e) As short as possible according to orders in queue. In this scheme, the product typically is fully manufactured after the customer order is received, according to the unique specifications of the customer. Order cycle is variable; it is specific for each situation, according to customer orders in queue.

f) Variable, as shortest as possible. In this scheme, there typically aren't significant quantities of customer orders in queue, and the order cycle depends of the length of time required to design the solution, adapt the processes, and produce the product or solution.

Minimum Order Quantity describes the minimum order quantity policy (i.e., minimum customer order size in terms of order value, transportation batch, and/or production batch).

a) Customer replenishment needs. In this instance, there is no minimum order size policy. Order size is based on customer replenishment needs.

b) Minimum economic production batch. This is useful when a product is produced according to unique specifications. Consequently, the customer must order the full quantity of the production batch.

c) Minimum economic transportation batch. This is useful when transportation costs are highly relevant in total cost. Consequently, the customer must order a full truck load or a minimum order value.

d) Minimum economic production batch or Minimum economic transportation batch. Company selects for each case, the greater of minimum economic production batch and minimum economic transportation batch, in order to assure the optimum batch for each specific case.

e) End consumer needs or customer replenishment needs. There is no minimum order size policy. This is useful when production is oriented to the end consumer (generally order size is one unit). When production is oriented to customers, order size is based on customer replenishment needs.

f) Collection pre-order. In this instance, minimum order size is determined according to the forecast defined by the customer for the collection. Minimum order size is determined according to customer pre-order of the season or collection.

Managerial Focus

Managerial Focus represents the linkage and alignment between an organization's competitive positioning and its Supply Chain Processes. The decision-making process on the daily activities governs the alignment between these two perspectives, and a proper set of policies ensures the coherence between strategies an execution.

Probably this is the most important factor for aligning supply chain with business strategy; however, companies do not pay attention to the definition of these policies, loosing coherence between business execution, making-decision process and business strategy.

Five policies comprise the managerial focus: end-to-end, service design, product design, transformation processes, and supplier's management.

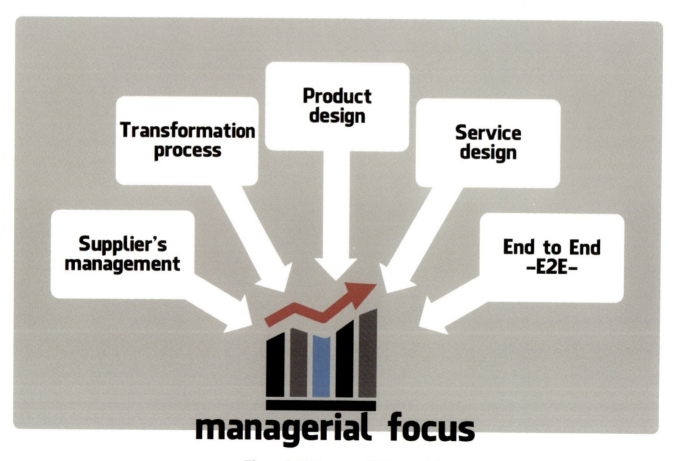

Figure 3.11 Factors of Managerial Focus

E2E (end-to-end) focus describes the main focus of the management of the end-to-end supply chain used in order to define the main criteria to make decisions and execute day-to-day operations. In order to define the proper selection of the pattern used for this policy, it is important to answer these questions:

- What is the main focus of the end-to-end supply chain?
- What is the main criterion to design the supply chain?

a) Collaborative relationships to build synergies. Such relationships are used when the company is oriented to establish collaborative programs with key customers in order to create synergies oriented to increase service level, reduce costs, and create value in both sides.

b) Efficiency. This policy is used when the supply chain is oriented to ensure the highest possible rate of use of assets in order to ensure the lowest product cost.

c) Continuous portfolio renewal. Such renewal applies if the organization is oriented to change in a fast and a continuous way its portfolio of products, i.e., developing SKUs with short lifetime in the market, and/or collection products.

d) Product configurability. This applies when the company is oriented to manufacture components that could be configured (assembled and/or finished) in infinite combinations, according to the preferences of each specific customer.

e) Adaptability to demand. This applies when the company's UVP is to offer the highest capacity of response to demand variations, either in customized products, changes in quantities, and/or requirement of delivery in lead-time shorter than your regular service policy.

f) Process adaptability. This applies when the company's main focus is to have flexible processes that could be reconfigured in different production flows according to a specific design of process and product for each specific customer order.

Service design describes the main focus of the customer service in order to define the main criteria to make decisions and execute day-to-day operations. In order to define the proper selection of the pattern used for this policy it is important to answer these questions:

- What is the main focus of service processes?
- What is the main criterion to design interface with customers?

a) Understanding and adaptability to customer needs. This pattern is used when the company is oriented to understand the specific requirement of the customer for each unique order; therefore, designing a specific solution for each order and providing customized solutions is a main attribute of its service.

b) Short lead-time. This applies when the company is oriented to ensure the shortest lead-time to response to customer orders in order to provide a fast response as a main attribute of its service.

c) Order accuracy. This applies when friendly and accurate customer order entry is the main focus of service. This approach is useful when the company serves customized requirements on massive segments.

d) Short time from idea to market. This applies when the main attribute of the service is to offer innovative and/or renewed products in a continuous way.

e) Perfect order fulfillment. This applies when the main attribute of the service is to ensure compliance of customer orders, in terms of quantity (fill rate), delivery (on time), and quality (e.g., commercial documents such as invoices, packing list, etc., and product specifications and product packaging according to customer requirements).

f) Information sharing for continuous improvement. This applies when the company is focused in to reduce demand uncertainties and increase synergies with customers. Consequently, the company shares information with its customers, such as through electronic orders, sales and inventory data, forecasting, new products introduction, market trends, etc.

Product design describes the main focus of the product design in order to define the main criteria to make decisions and execute day-to-day operations. In order to define the proper selection of the pattern used for this policy it is important to answer this question:

- What is the main focus of product design?

a) Designed for fast changeover & quick manufacturability. This pattern applies when product design is oriented to reduce production time per unit in order to reduce batch sizes and optimize inventory without detriment of productivity.

b) Fast product development process. This pattern is useful when product design is oriented to reduce time of product development (shorter time of product and process design) in order to increase rate of renewal of portfolio

c) Designed for small batches. This pattern applies when main focus is to design products oriented to minimize minimum economic production batch in order to allow the production of a large number of SKUs in small quantities for each.

d) Low cost at standard performance. This pattern is used when products are developed at the lowest total cost, ensuring a minimum performance level in order to obtain the lowest possible cost of the product.

e) Modular design for multiple configurations. This pattern applies when the main focus is to offer infinite configurations of products that are assembled or transformed from a unique platform of common components in order to take advantage of the postponement approach.

f) Supported by complimentary services. This pattern is recommended when the main focus is to offer value-added services supporting the product, such as in the design of product, design and manufacturing of unique spare parts, the specialized repair of equipment, or the implementation of fast solutions for unexpected situations.

Transformation process describes the main focus of the capacity management at the production processes in order to define the main criteria to make decisions and execute day-to-day operations.

a) High rate of asset utilization. This applies when the company is oriented to increase overall equipment efficiency (OEE), i.e., increase hours of effective utilization of assets, consequently, optimizing production and product cost.

b) Regular basis schedule in an optimal sequence of products. This applies when the company is oriented to hold a fixed sequence of production (SKU A first, SKU C, SKU Z, … SKU D…. and again, SKU A, SKU C, SKU Z … SKU D, etc.) in order to reduce variants of matrix of changeover, increasing ability for changeover, reducing changeover time, and, consequently, reducing production cycle (time required to produce the whole portfolio of products) in order to reduce batch sizes and optimize inventory without detriment of productivity and service.

c) High rate of assets utilization + capacity pooling for peaks. This pattern is used when installed capacity is defined by the average of the requirement at the lowest periods of demand. Peaks are supported by external capacity (third parties). This approach is useful in order to maintain the highest rate of use of own assets, with the flexibility of having additional capacity from third parties, without incurring fixed costs for non-use of that additional capacity.

d) Extra-capacity in manufacturing and downstream processes. This approach is recommended when the company is oriented to have a high capacity of response for peak of demand in order to provide the highest response level to customer's requirements.

e) High rate of asset utilization before PDP, and extra-capacity in PDP and downstream. This approach is useful when the company applies a postponement approach, in which the main proposal before PDP is to increase OEE and the main proposal in PDP and subsequent processes is to have high capacity of response for peaks of demand.

f) Assets flexibility and capacity pooling. This approach is recommended for companies oriented to have flexible assets, which are combined in unique flows according to the requirements of each specific customer order. Examples include metalworking workshops in which the machines are used according to the specifications and process designs of each customer order or modular sewing workshops in which the machines are configured and located in cells according to the requirements of the design of each specific garment.

Sourcing describes the main focus of the supplier management in order to define the main criteria to make decisions and execute day-to-day operations. For defining the proper pattern it is important to answer two questions:

- What is the main driver of the relationships with suppliers?
- What is the main criterion for selection of suppliers?

a) Innovativeness. This applies when the company's portfolio requires the newest and most innovative raw materials and components offered at the market in order to offer the newest and innovative portfolio to customers.

b) Lowest cost supplier. This is useful when raw materials and/or components are commodities. Consequently, the company is oriented to an opportunistic approach, choosing the best-cost supplier each time and optimizing the product cost.

c) Agile response to changes in demand. This applies when the demand profile is highly variable and a high response capacity is needed from suppliers in order to enhance the company's responsiveness without increasing inventory.

d) Collaborative relationships to build synergies. This applies when the company is oriented to eliminate redundant activities and to create synergies with suppliers in order to optimize service, cost, and/or value generation with the suppliers.

e) Shortest lead-time. This applies hen the company is oriented to hold a low inventory level of raw materials and components; consequently, it is important to obtain a short lead-time from suppliers.

f) Process flexibility to adapt to customer requirements. This applies when the company is focused in process flexibility, and so it is necessary to involve suppliers in this initiative in order to ensure end-to-end flexibility for creating unique solutions for each customer requirement.

Chapter 04
Common Patterns

A recommended arrangement of some tactical factors of the supply chain in order to avoid common pitfalls

Tool 2: 10 Common Patterns

Common Patterns are relationships among factors of the supply chain strategy. These rules must be followed in order to avoid basic mistakes, which cause major misalignments between supply chain and business strategy.

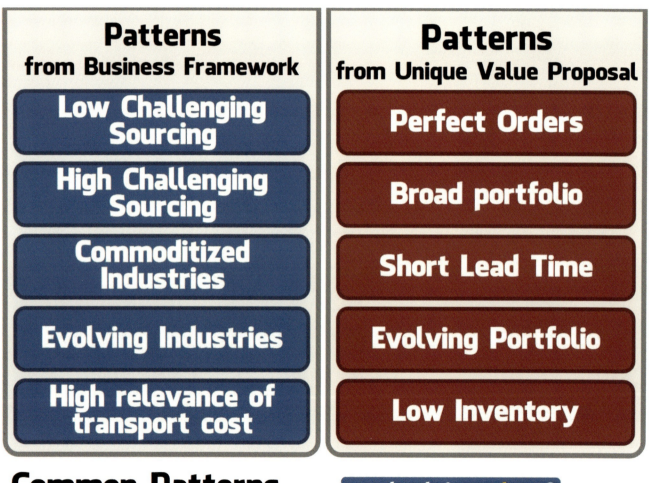

Figure 4.1 The 10-Common-Patterns

Common Pattern 1: Industries in a Low-Challenging Sourcing Pattern

A "low challenging sourcing" pattern is simultaneously characterized by:

Relevance of sourcing in the cost is high, which means materials or components purchased from suppliers are highly relevant in industry's cost structure.

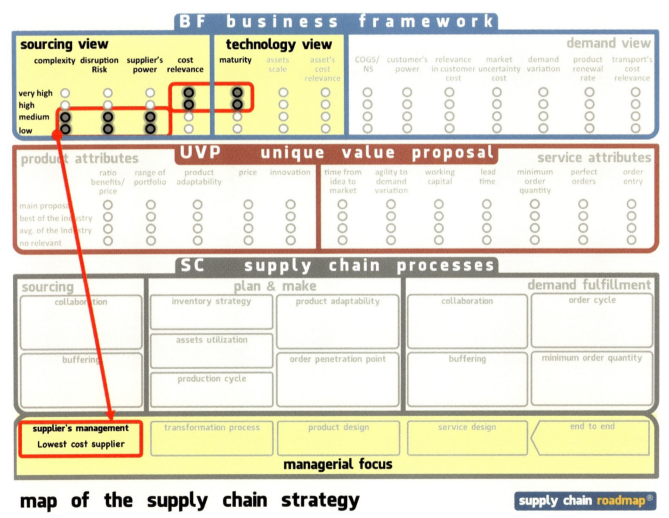

Figure 4.2 Common Pattern 1: Industries in a Low Challenging Sourcing

Technological maturity is high, innovation is infrequent and, when present, is incremental, meaning there are no major changes in the technology associated with materials or components.

Complexity is low, characterized by a few number of SKUs and suppliers and short lead-time for sourcing.

Disruption risk is low, and there is minimal or absent risk of shortage of sourcing.

Supplier's power is low as a consequence of excess of supply and multiple bidders in the market.

When an industry faces this pattern, sourcing tends to commoditization; therefore, the focus of the relationship with suppliers is an opportunistic approach looking at every purchase at the lowest possible cost, as shown in Figure 4.2.

Common Pattern 2: Industries in a High-Challenging Sourcing Position

A "high challenging sourcing" pattern is defined by the simultaneity presence of:

Complexity is high, characterized by a high number of sourced SKUs (materials, components, or products) or multiplicity of suppliers and long lead-time for sourcing. A high number of sourced SKUs is critical in industries in which a common platform of components (raw materials, semiprocessed parts, or finished parts) is used for the production of a high number of SKUs due to the shortage of one component or one supplier and could create a production stoppage.

In addition, long lead-time is another factor of high complexity, because long lead-time reduce the responsiveness to demand changes, creating a risk of sourcing shortage generated by higher consumption of components.

Disruption risk is high, due to a high demand of sourcing and lack of alternative sourcing (i.e., other suppliers or substitute materials).

Supplier's power is high as a consequence of shortage of supply into the market, which creates an unbalance into the commercial relationship and can potentially cause increased prices and poor service.

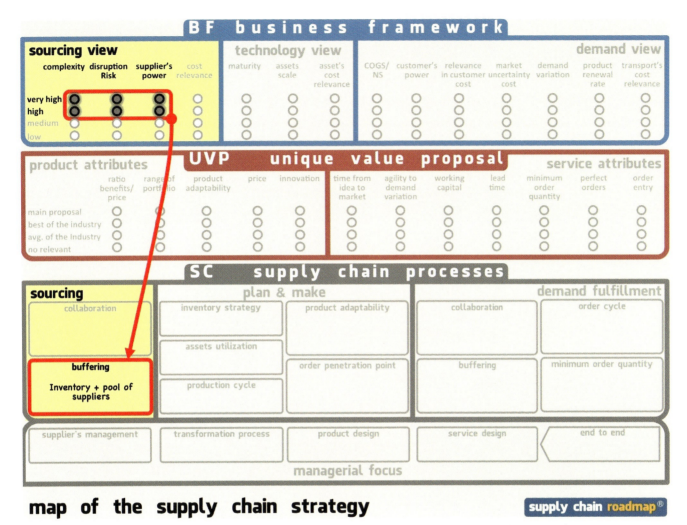

Figure 4.3 Common Pattern 2: Industries in a High Challenging Sourcing

When this pattern is present, risk of sourcing shortage is high. As a result, it is recommended to buffer sourcing with a pool of suppliers and high inventory levels of sourced components or materials, as is shown in Figure 4.3.

Generally, sourcing has cycles of capacity surplus and capacity deficit. When the cycle is in capacity surplus, power is on the side of the industry and agreements are favorable to the industry. When the cycle is in capacity deficit, the risk of sourcing shortage is high. Therefore, before defining sourcing buffering approach, it is critical to understand the current cycle of the industry.

The high-challenging sourcing pattern could have a more complex situation. When companies face a low-challenging sourcing pattern, they might make long term sourcing agreements with a very favorable price from suppliers. However, when the demand–supply cycle circles back, demand exceeds supply and power returns to suppliers. In this case, it could be unfavorable to maintain previous agreements with favorable prices because suppliers could be oriented to maximize revenue, giving priority to more profitable customers, therefore creating a high risk of shortage. In this case, buffering should be increased until new agreements with suppliers could be reached.

Common Pattern 3: "Commoditized" Industries

An industry is in a "commoditized" Business Framework when the following factors are present:
- Maturity level is very high, there are no major innovations in the industry, and brand equity is similar among competitors.
- Industry is oriented to increase the scale of assets in order to reduce significance of allocated cost (fixed and indirect cost).
- Despite higher productivity of the industry, gross margin is reduced by lower product prices.
- Demand and supply balance is on surplus and there are no significant differences in the product attributes among the industry, increasing power of the customers.

When product is the most important or one of the most important components in the client's cost structure, customers are oriented to look for alternative sourcing in order to reduce price. A common initiative of customers is to encourage the entry of new players into the industry or auctioning the sourcing, thereby increasing the competition into the industry and, consequently, reducing market prices.

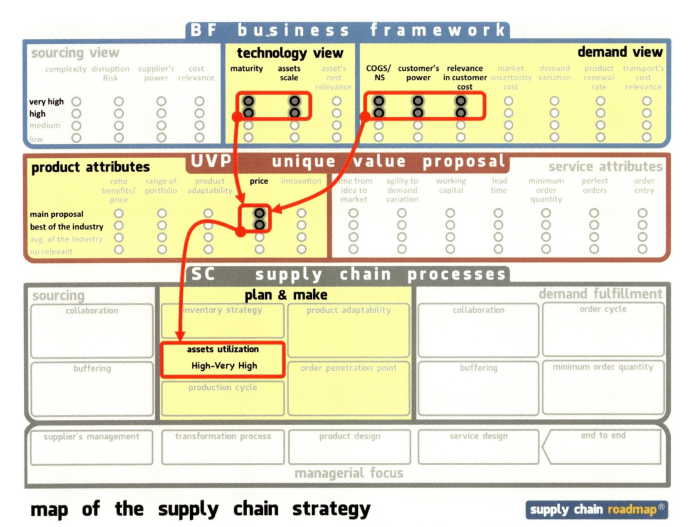

Figure 4.4: Common Pattern 3: Efficiency in Commoditized Industries

In an industry with a commoditized Business Framework, the UVP requires a lower price as a key attribute under client's perspective. As a result, the supply chain must maximize the utilization of assets to the detriment of the level of inventories and the length of the production cycle, as shown in Figure 4.4.

Common Pattern 4: "Evolving" Industries

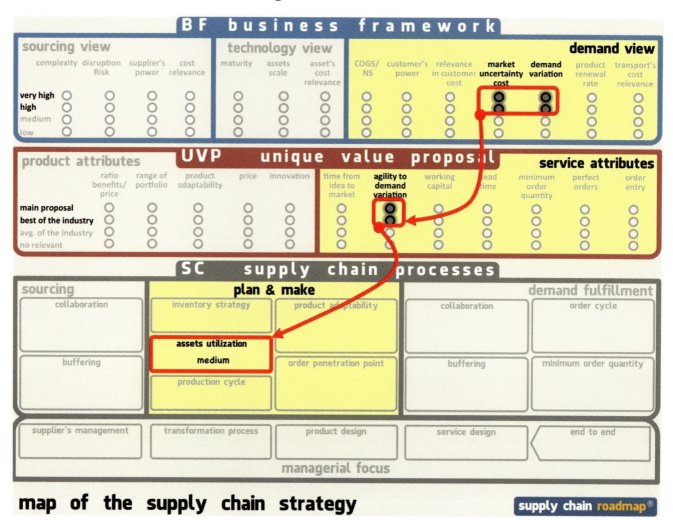

Figure 4.5: Common Pattern 4: Agility in Evolving industries.

An industry is in an "evolving" Business Framework when the following factors are present:

Market uncertainty costs are high; products are changing continuously due to fashion, technological developments or changing consumer habits; and, therefore, predictability of sales at SKU level is low, thus creating shortage of successful products and stock excess of unsuccessful products.

Demand variation is high, as a consequence of a high market uncertainty cost.

The value proposal recommended for this pattern requires agility to demand variation, which is characterized by excess capacity in order to increase responsiveness to demand changes, reducing risk of shortage/excess of inventory. Therefore, agility to demand reduces asset's utilization, minimizes the inventory level, and shortens the length of the production cycle, as shown in Figure 4.5.

Common Pattern 5: UVP Geared to Low Inventory

In an effort to achieve an advantage over the competition, some customers could be oriented to optimize inventory levels in order to increase working capital efficiency and reduce inventory holding cost.

This behavior is a consequence of high relevance of the product in the customer's cost structure and a mature sales and operations planning process. As a consequence, the industry should include in its value proposal a low working-capital attribute, which requires a high level of collaboration with the customer in order to have a mutual understanding of supply and demand.

When demand variation is high, it is not recommended to offer a low working-capital attribute because the industry should assume high levels of inventory in order to fulfill the customer's demand.

This common pattern could be useful for companies in commoditized industries, in order to move competition from a proposition of low prices to a "total value" proposal, introducing working capital and inventory holding as a key components of the total cost of the product under customer perspective.

Figure 4.6 shows the map of this pattern.

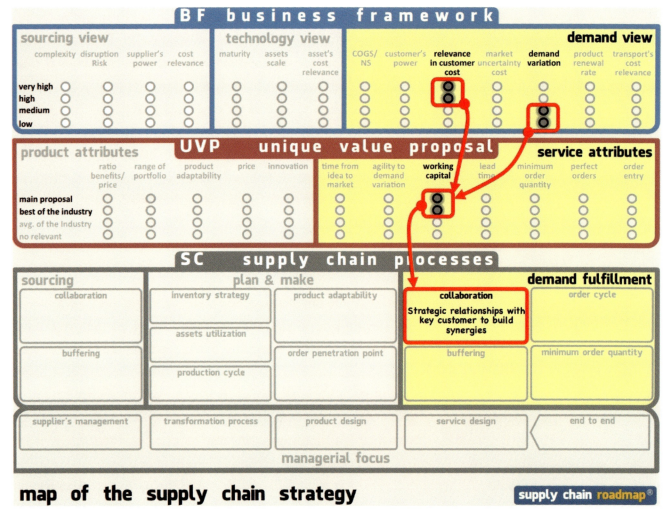

Figure 4.6: Common Pattern 5: Customer geared to low inventory.

Common Pattern 6: UVP Geared to Perfect Orders

When the UVP provides for perfect orders and/or a friendly and efficient order entry process, it is important to develop a collaborative program with customers in order to enhance mutual understanding and to create joint processes in order to align service policies, synchronize activities supporting the order to cash process, and eliminate redundancies and nonvalue-added processes, as shown in Figure 4.7.

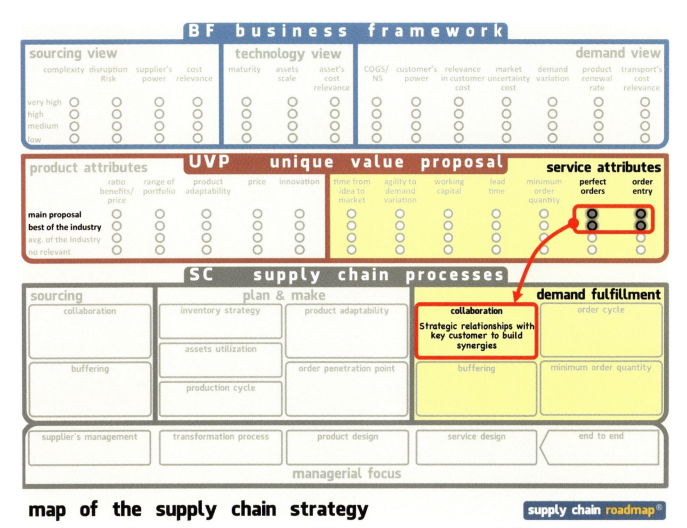

Figure 4.7: Common Pattern 6: UVP geared to perfect orders and efficient order entry

Common Pattern 7: UVP Offers a Broad Portfolio

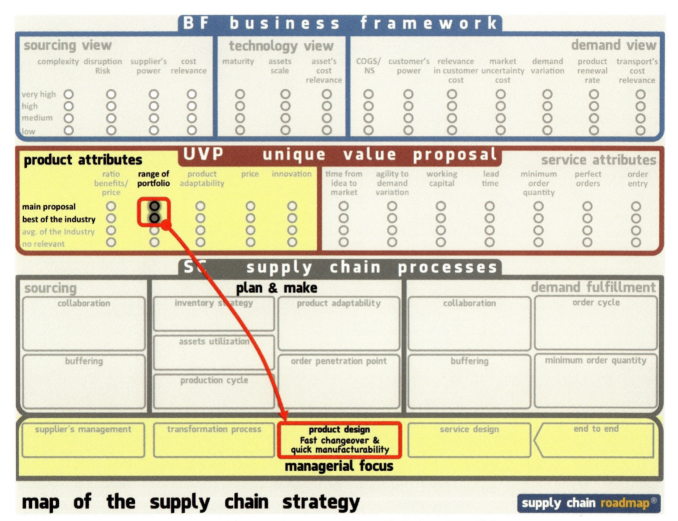

Figure 4.8 Common Pattern 7: A Broad Portfolio

When companies offers as a part of their UVP a broad product portfolio, and the assets are not specialized (i.e., the same asset is used to manufacture multiple SKUs in order to minimize the loss of efficiency in the use of assets), product design should be focused on quick changeover in order to reduce the negative impact on the use of assets, as shown in Figure 4.8.

Common Pattern 8: UVP Offers Short Lead Times

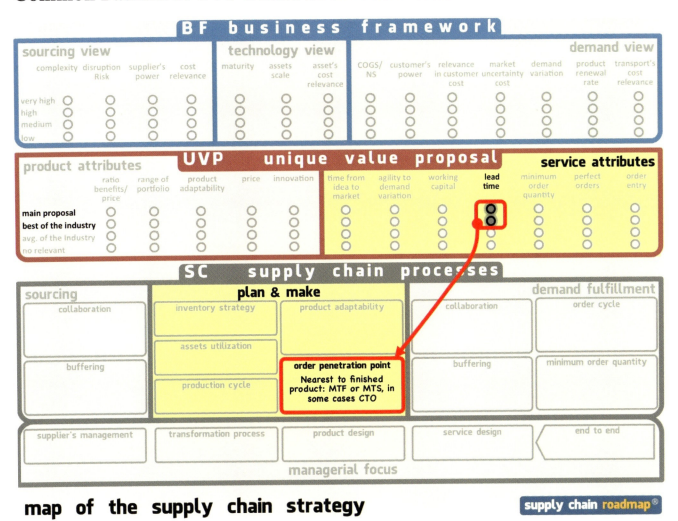

Figure 4.9 Common Pattern 8: Short Lead-time

A high-level attribute of shortest lead-time requires the OPP to be as close as possible to finished product inventory; thus, MTS or MTF is recommended because OPP doesn't require product processing after receiving customer order. Consequently, product dispatch could be started at the same moment when a fixed lead-time policy is defined or postponed until the next cycle or when a fixed cycle policy is agreed upon.

When product's customization is required, a MTS or MTF OPP are not viable, in this case is recommendable to take advantage of the postponement (a CTO OPP), in order to offer product customization reducing the lengthening of the lead-time as much is possible.

Figure 4.9 shows the recommended guidelines for the Common Pattern.

Common Pattern 9: High Relevance of Transport Costs

Generally high relevance of the cost of the product in the customer's cost structure requires a best price attribute. In an environment in which high transport costs relevance is present, a policy of no requiring a minimum size of order becomes irrelevant, and should be defined a minimum order size in order to ensure the best price as main attribute under customer's perspective, and consequently a full truckload minimum size order is recommended, as shown in Figure 4.10.

This is a policy that generates great controversies within organizations due that a no minimum order size policy is associated as a key component of a high service, however, this policy could be cause of inefficiency on transport, increasing the distribution cost, which directly or indirectly will be paid by the customers.

As an alternative, a proper definition of the minimum order size should be supported by a menu of tiered pricing for customers, according to the size of order placed by a customer. An analogous case of this policy is the cost of the delivery for e-commerce, where the cost of a delivery could be in a range for free to tens of dollars, according to the lead-time required by the customer.

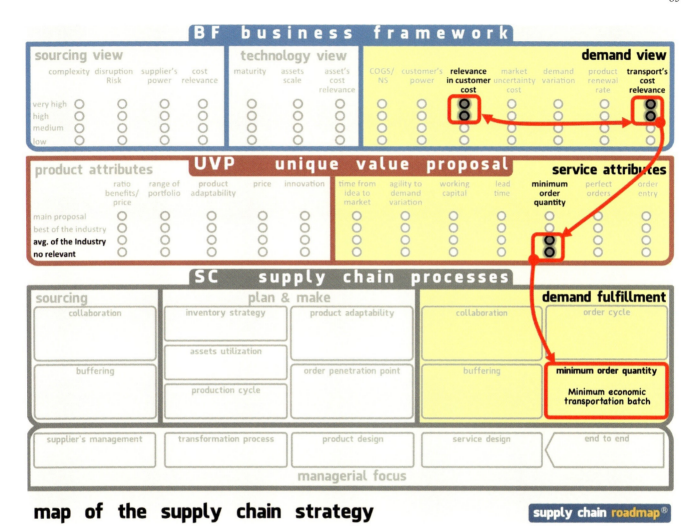

Figure 4.10 Common Pattern 9: High Relevance of Transportation Cost

Common Pattern 10: Evolving Portfolio

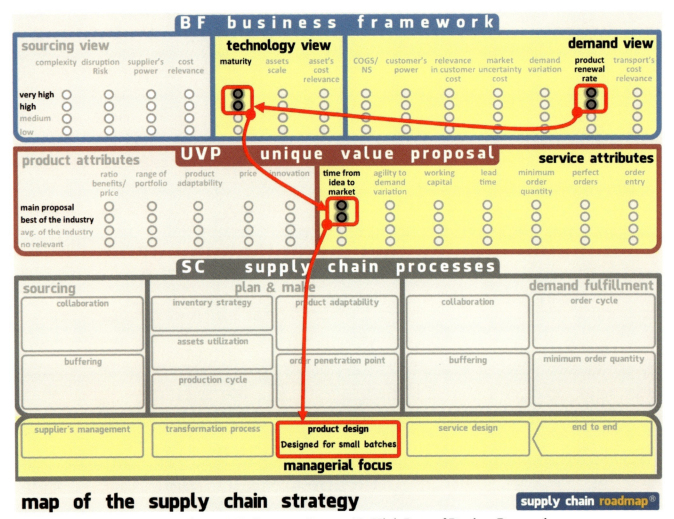

Figure 4.11 Common Pattern 10: High Rate of Product Renewal

This pattern is present when an industry is characterized by high product renewal rate and high technology maturity. In order to maintain a fresh and updated portfolio in the eyes of the customer, this pattern requires an update rate of the portfolio at a velocity greater than that required in other business environments. Consequently, the attribute time from idea to market should be at least in the average of the industry, which requires product design focused on product manufactured in small production batches in order to reduce market uncertainty cost. Figure 4.11 illustrates this Common Pattern.

Chapter 05
Supply Chain Archetypes

An original model of supply chain strategy worthy of imitation

Tool 3: Supply Chain Archetypes

A Supply Chain Archetype is a design pattern of the supply chain, which defines the key factors of the Business Framework, the relevant attributes of the UVP, and how to perform the design factors of the Supply Chain Processes, ensuring the alignment of the supply chain with the organization's competitive strategy. Other supply chains can be copied, modeled, or emulated from this prototype.

Once a company visualizes its supply chain strategy in the map (Tool 1) and understands the factors driving its supply chain, then it can determine which of six common Supply Chain Archetypes identified by the Supply Chain Roadmap best matches those criteria. These six are grouped in two categories: Supply Chain Archetypes that are driven by efficiency, and those that are driven by responsiveness. Archetypes will be used as role models in order to fill gaps in a company's supply chain strategy.

Supply Chain Archetypes Driven by Efficiency

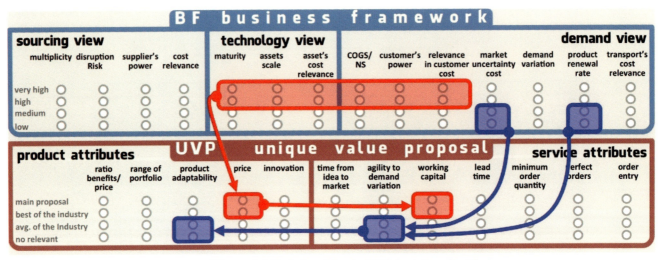

Figure 5.1 Relationships in Efficient Supply Chains

Efficient supply chains are characterized by two main relationships among the Business Framework and the UVP, which are shown in Figure 5.1

The Business Framework shows simultaneously the presence of factors oriented to commoditized industries: mature technology, assets of big scale, assets highly relevant in total cost, low gross margin, customers with multiple choices which increase customers' power, and products highly relevant in the customer's cost structure. These factors push the UVP to high dependence on both low prices and low working capital.

On the other hand, the Business Framework shows a low relevance of factors as product renewal rate and market uncertainty cost, thus requiring no product customization and, consequently, reducing the need of agile response to demand variation.

These relationships drive the value proposal toward low cost and/or high relevance of asset utilization to total cost. Consequently, end-to-end efficiency is a must. These behaviors are common in industries such as cement, steel, paper, commodities, and low-cost fashion, among others. They are best suited to one of three supply chain types—efficient, fast, or continuous-flow—that are best able to maximize asset utilization, which will be explained below.

The Efficient Supply Chain Archetype

An efficient supply chain is focused on maximizing the use of productive assets as a key element to achieve a competitively priced product. Despite this, the Archetype is widely mentioned by several authors, some of whom called the model lean, which is a recognizable term in the industry. But it is misused because the real lean model was developed by Toyota in 1950s and is a mix of agile and efficient models. Although an efficient model uses a make-to-forecast order penetration point, Toyota Production System uses an assembly to order penetration point. Misunderstanding may have originated in the fact that both models are oriented to lowest total cost. But a lean supply chain must not be confused with lean management, which should be understood as a management model that could be overlapped over any supply chain model in order to improve business performance.

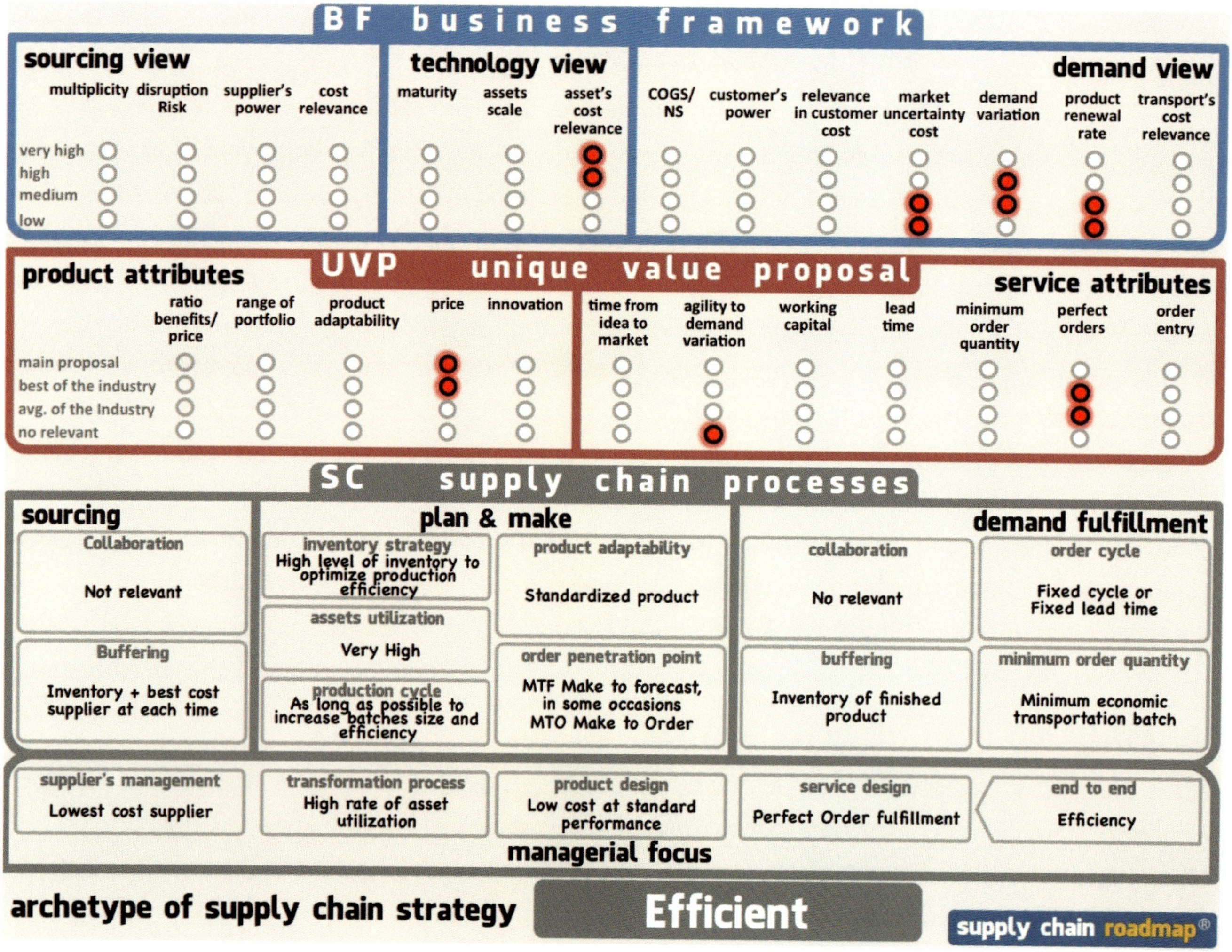

Figure 5.2 Efficient Supply Chain Archetype

Figure 5.2 shows the map of the efficient Supply Chain Archetype, in which the relevant factors and their characterization are visible.

The Business Framework of the efficient supply chain is characterized by a product renewal rate that is very low (i.e., stable products, which, with minor changes such as packaging and minor benefits, remain on the market for long periods of time) because products are commoditized. This means that products have low differences among the suppliers (the industry) and/or several alternative substitute are available to customers; therefore, the customer's power is high.

Consequently, customers have an opportunistic behavior (i.e., looking for the best price, avoiding long-term relationships), which manifests itself in a retention of the orders until the end of the month, with the aim of obtaining better commercial conditions given the industry's need to fulfill his own sales plan. Therefore, the industry perceives a high variation of the demand (i.e., end-of-month syndrome), under which a major portion of the dispatches of the month are realized in a very few days.

Another important factor in the Business Framework of the efficient Supply Chain Archetype is the relevance of assets in the total cost. When this factor is very high, there are not options, and it is mandatory to maximize efficiency. In such a case, the efficient supply chain pattern is the right choice.

When this factor is on high level or below, efficient Archetype could be an option, but it is not mandatory and could be a better option look for other patterns where competition is based on other attributes different than price, looking for a less fiery competition on the market.

The UVP of an efficient supply chain is characterized by an agility to demand that is practically absent, because agility requires extra capacity and its detriments the utilization of the assets, and, consequently the efficiency. Instead, price becomes in the most relevant attribute around which customers make purchase decisions. After price, price is the most important consideration for customers. Perfect orders become the next most important attribute, which should be at least at the average of the industry.

In essence, the efficient supply chain is best suited to industries characterized by intense market competition, where several competitors are fighting for the same group of customers who may not perceive major differences in their value proposals. In effect, competition is based almost solely on price.

It is important to consider several factors when implementing the efficient Supply Chain Archetype. First, supplier's management should be focused on an opportunistic approach in order to take advantage of the best cost at each moment. Consequently, sourcing buffering should have enough inventory levels in order to secure power and, therefore, control of the relationship with the supplier. If inventory level is low, suppliers could recover power based on the risk of disruption of supply.

Because customers in these commoditized businesses take an opportunistic approach to purchasing in order to ensure that they get the best price for each order, it results in a demand profile with recurrent peaks, which creates high variation of the demand. Consequently, a continuous-replenishment product flow is inappropriate. Production should instead be scheduled based on sales expectations for the length of the production cycle, using a model based on a make to forecast order penetration point, in order to maintain production continuity, and reduce set up time; which implies production of standardized products in an optimal scheduling based on the forecast.

A make-to-forecast production is performed before orders are received based on a detailed planning of production activities in order to ensure focus on efficiency. In high- or medium-scale industries, inventory and production cycles could be on opposite sides of the efficiency spectrum, because, for the efficient pattern, inventory strategy maximizes assets utilization in detriment of inventory level and production cycle. Larger production cycles increase production batches, and, therefore, asset utilization is higher, but inventory levels are high because the cycle inventory is larger.

Demand fulfillment is characterized by a practical approach: (1) buffering supported by enough finished inventory; (2) minimum order quantity (MOQ) related to full truck load in order to ensure maximum load efficiency, and, (3) order cycle defined by lead-time.

A variation of the full truck load MOQ could be used when MOQ is defined by a half or a third of a full truck load for each customer and order cycle is changed to a fixed cycle, with the aim to consolidate two or three customers at the same truck on the same day.

Managerial focus should be on promoting maximum end-to-end efficiency. There are two main actions they can take to accomplish this. First, they should ensure high rates of asset utilization coupled with a high overall equipment efficiency (OEE) in order to reduce cost. Second, they should ensure high levels of forecast accuracy to guarantee product availability and, consequently, perfect order fulfillment.

Figure 5.3 shows the main relationships among the factors in this Archetype.

To be successful in this Supply Chain Archetype, several factors should be in place. First, there should be extra capacity in outbound logistics, with the purpose of absorbing demand peaks without affecting the ability to meet customers' expected receiving dates.

The SKU portfolio should be trimmed back to reduce the number of high-variation, low-demand SKUs, which create complexity in production and service.

The production cycle should be scheduled in a logical sequence of SKUs, with the aim of reducing setup time between each pair of adjacent SKUs. The production sequence should be fixed and maintained for long periods of time; this will help to increase the manufacturing line's experience with each setup, reducing the amount of time it takes for changeovers and, consequently, the length of the production cycle.

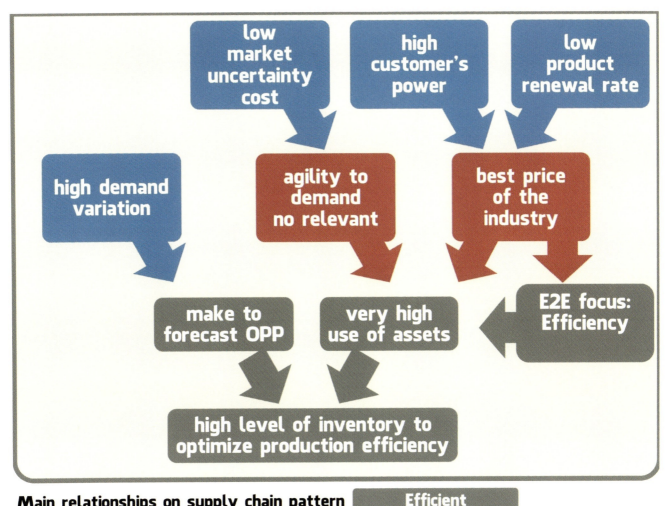

Figure 5.3: Main Relationships of Efficient Archetype

When transportation cost is highly relevant to the total cost, a minimum order-size policy of a full truckload is recommended. An alternative is a fixed order-cycle policy that allows the company to consolidate certain customers' orders on the same truck. For example, orders for customers in the northeast region are consolidated every Tuesday at 5 p.m. and are dispatched the next day.

When market demand evidences seasonal trends, extra warehousing capacity should be available in anticipation of the need to store additional product during high-demand periods.

Customers whose buying behavior follows a regular and predictable behavior should be invited to participate in collaborative programs, whereby supplier and customer share demand and supply forecasts and schedules in order to reduce demand variability. The purpose is to migrate them to a continuous-replenishment model, and then, step by step, to convert the supply chain model from efficient to continuous-flow (discussed later), which is a more mature Archetype that generates higher levels of customer loyalty.

This Supply Chain Archetype is well suited for businesses with commoditized products in an industry with high scale assets, such as cement and steel or for businesses oriented toward low-cost products. The Tata Nano, a vehicle produced in India for Tata Motor and oriented to low-income people, is a recent example of a supply chain oriented to efficiency. The Nano design premise was to manufacture a vehicle with the best retail price in the industry (US $2,500), meaning that its UVP was price. Suppliers were selected under a low-cost premise. Tata worked with their motorcycle suppliers to take advantage of the low cost of motorcycle components and then redesigned them for the Nano.

Tata takes advantage of maximize the assets utilization in order to minimize effect on fixed costs, providing assembly and painting services to third parties such as Mahindra and Mercedes-Benz. Suppliers were located in areas adjacent to the assembly plant in order to reduce logistics cost. The location of the plant in Singur was determined by seeking cheap labor and tax subsidies, before the arrival of Tata unemployment in this area was 47%, which, confirms that an efficient supply chain seeks efficiency from end to end.

The "Fast" Supply Chain Archetype

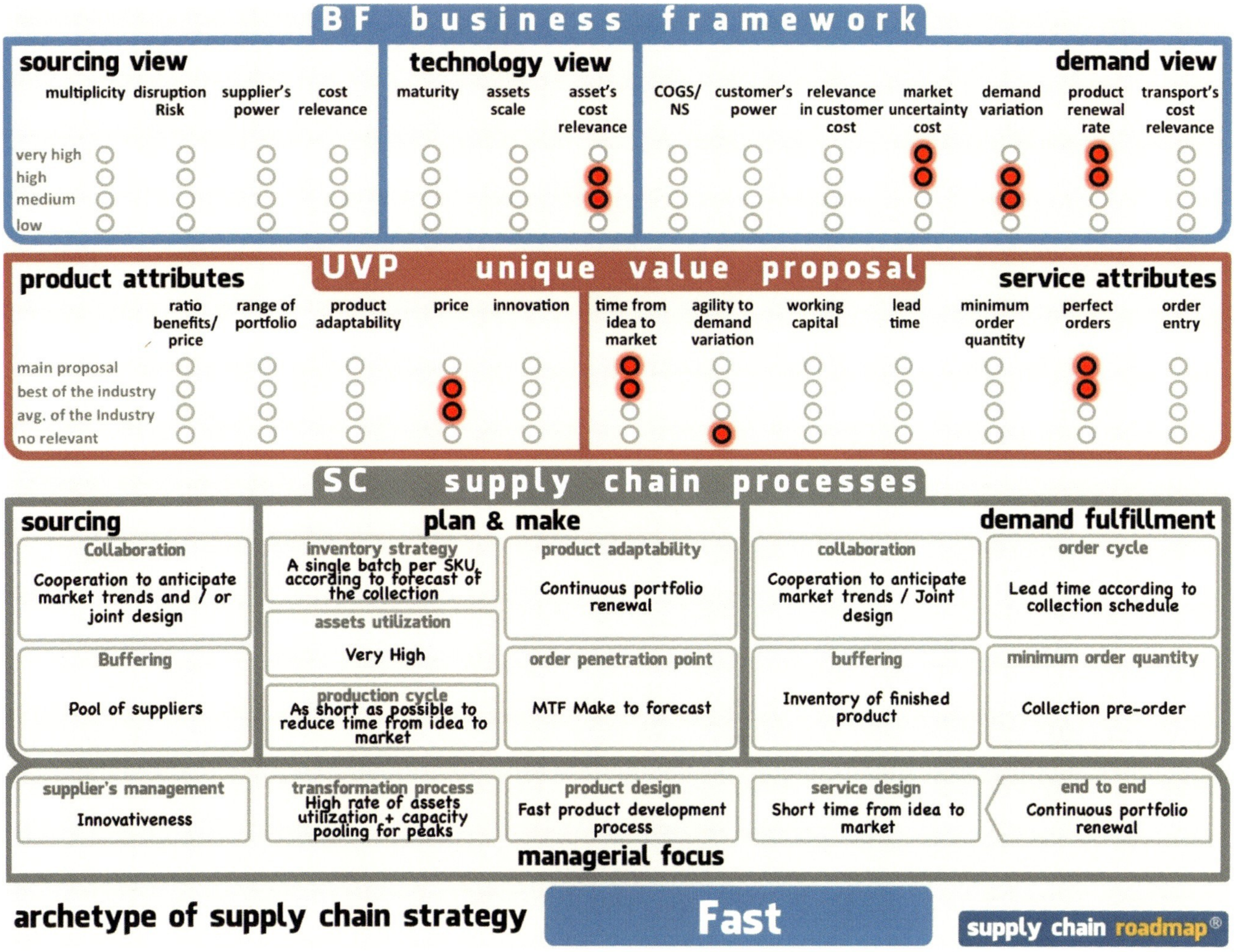

Figure 5.4 Fast Archetype

Within the group of supply chain driven by efficiency, the next Archetype is the fast supply chain, which, is characterized by a continuous and fast renewal of products framed in an efficient operation.

Figure 5.4 shows the map of supply chain strategy of the fast Archetype, in which the relevant factors and their characterization are visible.

The Business Framework of the fast Supply Chain Archetype is characterized by a product renewal rate that is very high because products are highly changing often due to fashion or technological changes or a combination of both. Such products have significant differences among the suppliers (the industry), reducing the customer's power.

Consequently, customer preferences have a changing behavior, and this behavior manifests itself in a high level variation of the demand, which is driven by the degree of success of the products. Therefore, the industry perceives a high market uncertainty cost, which manifests in the cost of lost sales of successful products, and the cost of price down and inventories write-off for unsuccessful products.

Another important factor in the Business Framework of the fast pattern is the relevance of assets in the total cost, which normally is high (in some cases medium), forcing the company to maximize efficiency in a complex production environment due to the continuous change of the SKUs.

On the other hand, in the UVP, the most relevant attribute is the time from idea to market, which, is a key requirement in order to maintain a renewed portfolio for the customers. Price also is a relevant attribute on which customers support the purchase decision. Consequently, prices should be at least in the average of the industry and preferably among the best of the industry.

Because such products have a short period of life, perfect orders becomes in an important attribute in order to ensure products are available for the customers at the right moment, especially when products are oriented to seasonal trends.

In essence, the fast supply chain is best for companies that produce trendy products with a short lifecycle. From the customer's perspective, the main difference among competitors' UVPs is how well they are able to update product portfolios in accordance with the latest trends. This focuses competition in the market on manufacturers' ability to continuously develop new products they can sell at an affordable price. As result, the main driver of competitiveness is the reduction of market-mediation costs. In an industry framework characterized by a short lifecycle, this might appear to be a conundrum, but based on an understanding of market trends and consumers' habits, market uncertainty cost could be maintained at an optimal level.

In the architecture of the supply chain for a fast pattern, it is important to consider several topics. First, supplier's management should be focused on a collaborative approach in order to anticipate market trends; however, as demand is highly variable, sourcing buffering should focused on maintaining a pool of suppliers in order to disperse the risk of disruption among several suppliers.

Because portfolio of products is in a continuous renewal, demand predictability could be low. Because of that, production should be scheduled based on sales expectations for the length of the sales season (normally short periods of a few weeks) using a model based on a make-to-forecast order penetration point. The foregoing implies that the fast Archetype has a product adaptability based on a continuous change of the portfolio from one season to another season, but producing standardized product within the same season, with the aim of maximizing production efficiency.

The plan and make dimension is driven by two main factors: inventory strategy driven by a single production batch per SKU, where the batch size per SKU is defined based on sales expectations for the sales season (or collection, in the fashion industry), and a short production cycle in order to reduce time to market.

Demand fulfillment dimension is characterized by a collection-oriented approach, where buffering is supported by finished inventory of the current collection, although responsiveness of buffering is low as consequence of the short life of the SKUs in order to reduce risk of obsolescence. On the other hand, minimum order quantity (MOQ) is related to collection preorder, and order cycle is defined by the collection schedule, which is driven by the time from idea to market; as the company reduces the time from idea to market, the order cycle is shorter. Normally, due to the short life of the collections, there are few dispatches by season (in some cases a unique dispatch for each season), but, in order to avoid supply oversizing, there isn't a minimum economic transportation batch's policy, which could generate product's obsolescence.

Managerial focus should be oriented on promoting continuous portfolio renewal, which is supported by three main capabilities: short time from idea to market, maximum levels of forecast accuracy in order to reduce market-uncertainty cost, and end-to-end efficiency in order to ensure affordable costs for customers. Figure 5.5 shows the main relationships among the factors of this Archetype.

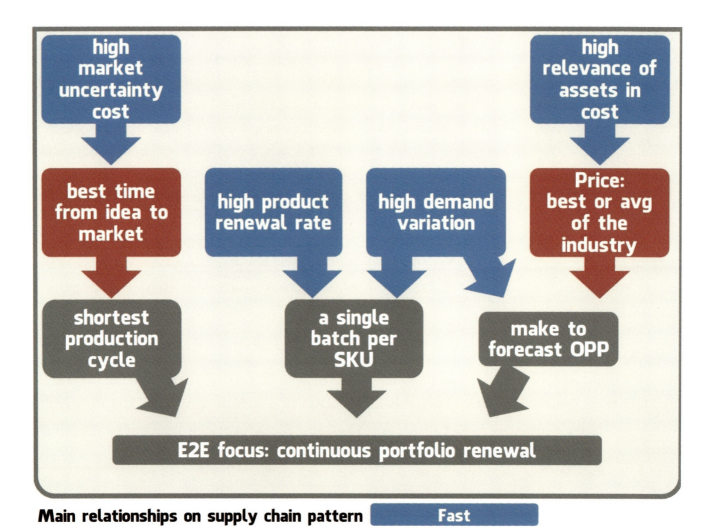

Figure 5.5: Main Relationships of Fast Archetype

For this Supply Chain Archetype to be successful, several factors should be in place. First, for companies with high levels of seasonal demand, there must be a pool of suppliers that can provide additional capacity as needed. Although outsourced manufacturing cost could be more expensive than in-house manufacturing, in the long term it would be less expensive than unused capacity.

Classic SKUs, defined as those that have a permanent presence in the product portfolio, should be replenished under a continuous-flow Supply Chain Archetype.

The fast Supply Chain Archetype is the most demanding in terms of forecast accuracy because it has to constantly anticipate market trends. This creates the highest level of market-mediation cost. Consequently, it requires the deployment of a sales and operations planning process supported by a state-of-the-art forecasting techniques.

Because product portfolios are extensive and change frequently, there will be many SKUs with low sales volumes. Therefore, it is crucial to develop the ability to produce small batches and to purchase sourced components in small quantities.

Modular processes and sharing of sourced components among several SKUs also help to ensure fast product development and manufacturability.

When a company slows the rate of portfolio renewal or lengthens the lifespan of its product collections or marketing campaigns, it should migrate to an efficient Supply Chain Archetype. This will allow it to reduce batch sizes and to manufacture based on several batches of the same SKU during the term of the collection or sales season.

As the sales season becomes shorter, demand fulfillment becomes more difficult because there isn't enough time to manufacture and replenish stock before the product goes out of fashion and consumers no longer want to buy it. For this reason, it is important to develop abilities oriented to reduce the time from idea to market. Some companies with a global presence manage this challenge by moving seasonal surplus from one market to other markets. However, due to global interconnection, consumer preferences toward to overlap at the same time among markets, reducing time frame for moving products surplus among markets.

Examples of companies that benefit from this Supply Chain Archetype include those that engage in catalog sales. Companies in this industry segment typically launch new marketing campaigns every three or four weeks, and each catalog may refresh more than 50 percent of the SKUs featured. It's also appropriate for retailers that sell trendy apparel and whose customers tend to visit stores monthly. These retailers need to revise their stores' SKU portfolio every few weeks so loyal customers see renewed inventory during each visit.

Zara, the Spanish garment company, is an iconic case in the fast Supply Chain Archetype. In their definition of value proposal, they estimate a customer visits the store every 20 or 30 days. They claim that during each visit, a customer could find a high renewal of the portfolio of the store, but with a prerequisite: affordable prices.

The core of Zara's success resides in the short time from idea to market. Zara is able to place in five weeks a new product in the store and redesigned products in just two weeks. How does Zara achieve the shortest time from idea to market?

Fabrics are bought raw and dyed and finished to the last minute.

Manufacture is oriented to small batches.

Production is according to a forecast of limited quantities to create a sense of scarcity and generate impulse buying.

Fast moving of the products along the supply chain, products don't spend more than three days in its distribution center located on Arteixo (Spain).

The "Continuous Flow" Supply Chain Archetype

The last Archetype of the group of supply chains driven by efficiency is the Continuous Flow supply chain, which is characterized by a continuous replenishment of product with the aim of optimizing working capital, framed in an efficient operation.

Figure 5.6 shows the map of supply chain strategy of the Archetype continuous flow, in which the relevant factors and their characterization are visible.

The Business Framework of the continuous-flow Supply Chain Archetype is characterized by two main factors: a very low product renewal rate because products are commoditized, which means that products have low differences among the suppliers (the industry) and/or there are several alternative substitute for the customers, and the product's holding costs, such as warehousing, financial cost of the inventory, insurances, etc., have high relevance in customer cost because customers are willing to hold a low inventory level.

High relevance of inventory holding cost drives customer to maintain a steady flow of product in order to avoid hidden cost, reducing demand variation.

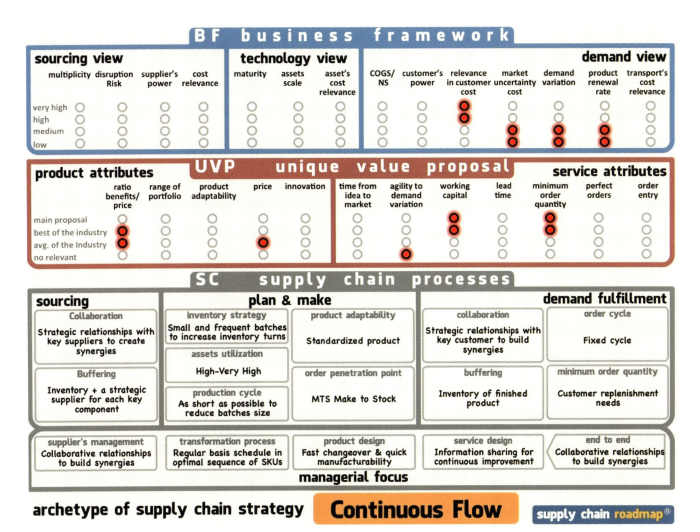

Figure 5.6 Continuous Flow Archetype

Market is mature and products are oriented to commoditization. Consequently, market uncertainty cost is low.

Regardless of the extent of the relevance of assets in the total cost, when a product's renewal rate and market uncertainty cost are low, and customers are not opportunistic, the continuous-flow

Archetype is the proper choice in order to maximize efficiency based on a high use of assets combined with a steady flow.

Similar to the efficient and fast Archetypes, the UVP of a Continuous Flow supply chain is characterized by a high relevance of price for the customer and, consequently, absence of agility to demand.

Price becomes a required attribute—a Order Qualifier—but it is not the most valued by customers.

Due to high inventory holding costs, working capital becomes the most important attribute in the eyes of customers, in order to avoid complexities related to high inventory level.

Despite the importance of working capital, customers won't be willing to reduce inventory level if their confidence in the supplier is low. As a result, perfect orders becomes the second most important attribute, without which customers won't agree to move to a sourcing relationship under a continuous-flow Archetype.

The main features of the continuous-flow Archetype are supply and demand stability, with processes scheduled in such way as to ensure a steady cadence and continuous flow of information and products. This Archetype typically is for a very mature supply chain with a customer demand profile that has little variation and for customers oriented to reduce inventory level.

In the architecture of the supply chain for a continuous-flow pattern, it is important to consider several topics. First, supplier's management should be focused on a collaborative approach oriented toward creating synergies that take advantage of the steady flow of product and information.

The UVP is based on offering a continuous-replenishment system to customers in order to ensure high service levels and low inventory levels at customers' facilities. Consequently, the production workload can match demand through a make-to-stock order penetration point, where production is scheduled to replenish predefined stock levels, which are defined based on a specified reorder point for inventory in the production cycle.

As was explained in the efficient Supply Chain Archetype, in high or medium scale industries, inventory and production cycles could be on the opposite side of the efficiency spectrum because, for the continuous-flow Archetype, inventory's strategy maximizes importance of short production cycle and low inventory level in detriment of assets utilization. However, it doesn't imply medium or low levels of assets utilization, because efficiency is supported in the development of abilities to produce small batches with low waste and short time for change of product, normally using single minute exchange die (SMED) techniques, which were developed by Shigeo Shingo in Japan in the 1950s and 1960s. SMED is a technique oriented to reduce to no more than 10 minutes the time from the manufacture of the last piece of a batch until obtaining a right part of the first following batch.

The above allow to offer a minimum-order-quantity policy related to customer's needs in each order and a short and fixed order cycle, which allows for the consolidation of demand of several customers for the same region in order to increase truckload filling efficiency.

Buffering is managed in the traditional way, supported by finished inventory.

Managerial focus should be to promote supply chain collaboration, which is supported by four main capabilities. In the early stages, they include electronic transactions used to reduce the number of transactional processes required during the order cycle, as well as the sharing of sales and inventory information to help increase the ability to predict demand. In the most mature stage, collaborative planning with key customers helps to anticipate demand patterns and looking for synergies in the shared supply chain. Figure 5.7 shows main relations among factors of the continuous flow Archetype.

To be successful in this Supply Chain Archetype, the following factors should be in place:

Companies should use a prescheduled order cycle—for example, receiving orders from a group of customers the same day every week—instead of a lead-time order cycle, in which orders are dispatched based on a fixed lead-time after order entry, independent of when an order is received. A lead-time order cycle could create demand peaks and thus break up the continuous flow.

High-variance SKUs should be buffered with higher levels of inventory in order to avoid unexpected changes in the production schedule.

The production cycle should be scheduled in a logical sequence of SKUs, with the aim of reducing setup time between each pair of adjacent SKUs. The production sequence should be fixed and maintained for long periods of time; this will help to increase the manufacturing line's experience with each setup, reducing the amount of time it takes for changeovers and, consequently, the length of the production cycle.

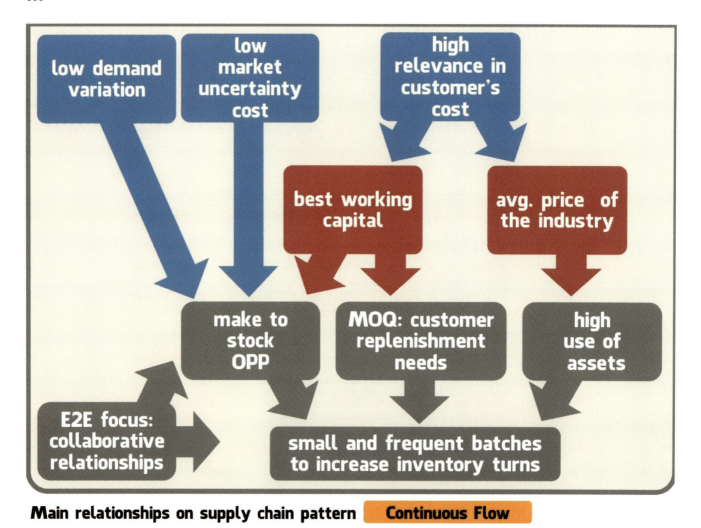

Figure 5.7 Main Relationships of Continuous Flow Archetype

Collaborative efforts should be oriented toward customers that generate higher sales and those with high demand variability. For the latter group, if demand variability continues even after participation in a collaborative program, then it would be advisable to evaluate their substitution for other customers because they are forcing the supply chain to increase inventory or to break up a production sequence, both of which affect supply chain efficiency.

When market-demand variability moves in irregular patterns and/or customers are moving toward an opportunistic approach—that is, they are looking for the best price without regard for other benefits, such as lower working capital—it is wise to consider migration to an efficient supply chain.

This Supply Chain Archetype typically works well for businesses with short-shelf-life products, such as dairy products and bread. It is also suitable for manufacturers of intermediate products, such as original equipment manufacturer (OEM) parts for assembly.

A good example is Bimbo, the Mexican bread manufacturer that works in Latin America and the United States. Bimbo replenishes the inventory of its customers continuously, reaching almost zero inventory policy on fresh product in their platforms and assuring a challenging value promise to the retailers: Products in the shelves have at least seven days before the expiration date or product is replaced without cost.

Comparison of Supply Chains Oriented to Efficiency

Figure 5.8 shows a comparison among the three Supply Chain Archetypes oriented to efficiency, where the main factors of the three perspectives and the typical qualification for each Archetype are shown.

The main distinctions among these Archetypes are caused by the differences on the market uncertainty cost and demand variation, which are higher on the fast Archetype. In the fast Archetype, the industry is highly affected by changes of consumer preferences, therefore requiring a short time for developing ideas and the introduction of products to market in order to ensure a continuous renewal of the product portfolio.

On the other hand, the efficient Archetype has a lower market uncertainty cost, which eliminates the need of a continuous portfolio renewal and consequently moves the industry to a high level of commoditization of product, whereby price becomes the main attribute and, thus, end-to-end efficiency is the focus of this Archetype.

Finally, maturity in relations with the distribution channel can reduce the demand variation. Consequently, migrating from an efficient Archetype to a continuous flow Archetype, in which remains the basis of a competitive price, and, in addition is offered as the main value proposal a high level of inventory rotation, reducing handling and financial costs of the inventory, and therefore providing a lower total cost to the customer.

		Continuous Flow	**Efficient**	**Fast**
Business Framework	Asset's cost relevance	Mainly High - Very High	High - Very High	Medium - High
	Market uncertainty cost	Low - Medium	Low - Medium	High - Very High
	Demand Variation	Low - Medium	Medium - High	Medium - High
Unique Value Proposal	Price	Average or Best	Best	Average or Best
	Agility to demand	No relevant	No relevant	No relevant
	Main Value Proposal	Working Capital Optimization	Price	Time from idea to market
Supply Chain Processes	Product Adaptability	Standardized Product	Standardized Product	Changing Product
	Inventory Strategy	Small & frequent batches to increase inventory turns	High level of inventory to optimize efficiency	A single batch per SKU, according to forecast of the collection
	Asset's utilization	High - Very High	Very High	High - Very High
	Order Penetration Point	Make to Stock	Make to Forecast	Make to Forecast
	Demand buffering	Inventory of finished product	Inventory of finished product	Inventory of finished product
	End to End Managerial Focus	Collaborative relationships to build synergies	End to End efficiency	Continuous Portfolio renewal

Figure 5.8 Comparison of Supply Chain Archetypes oriented to efficiency.

Supply Chains Oriented to Responsiveness

Responsive supply chains are characterized by two main relationships between Business Framework and Unique Value Proposal. Business Framework shows the presence of factors oriented to innovative industries: technology in development, low relevance of assets in total cost, and high gross margin. Consequently, low prices lose relevance for customers.

In addition, the Business Framework shows a high relevance of factors as product renewal rate, demand variation, and market uncertainty cost, increasing in the UVP the need for agile response to demand variation, high product adaptability, and a wide portfolio of products in order to reduce risks associated to market uncertainty cost.

Figure 5.9 shows the dominant relationships into the responsive supply chains.

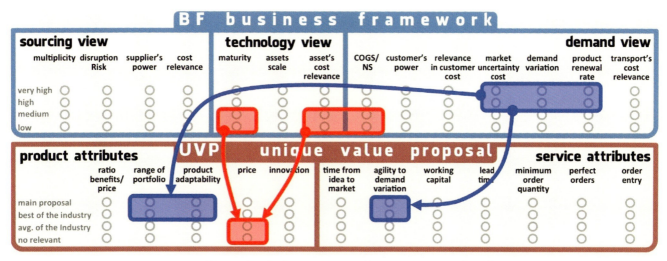

Figure 5.9 Relationships in Responsive Supply Chains

As discussed, industries that face considerable demand uncertainty, where market uncertainty cost is highly relevant (e.g., fashion, technology, and products with a high component of services), should employ one of three different supply chain approaches that are oriented toward providing capacity in response to changes in demand: agile, custom-configured, or flexible.

The Agile Supply Chain Archetype

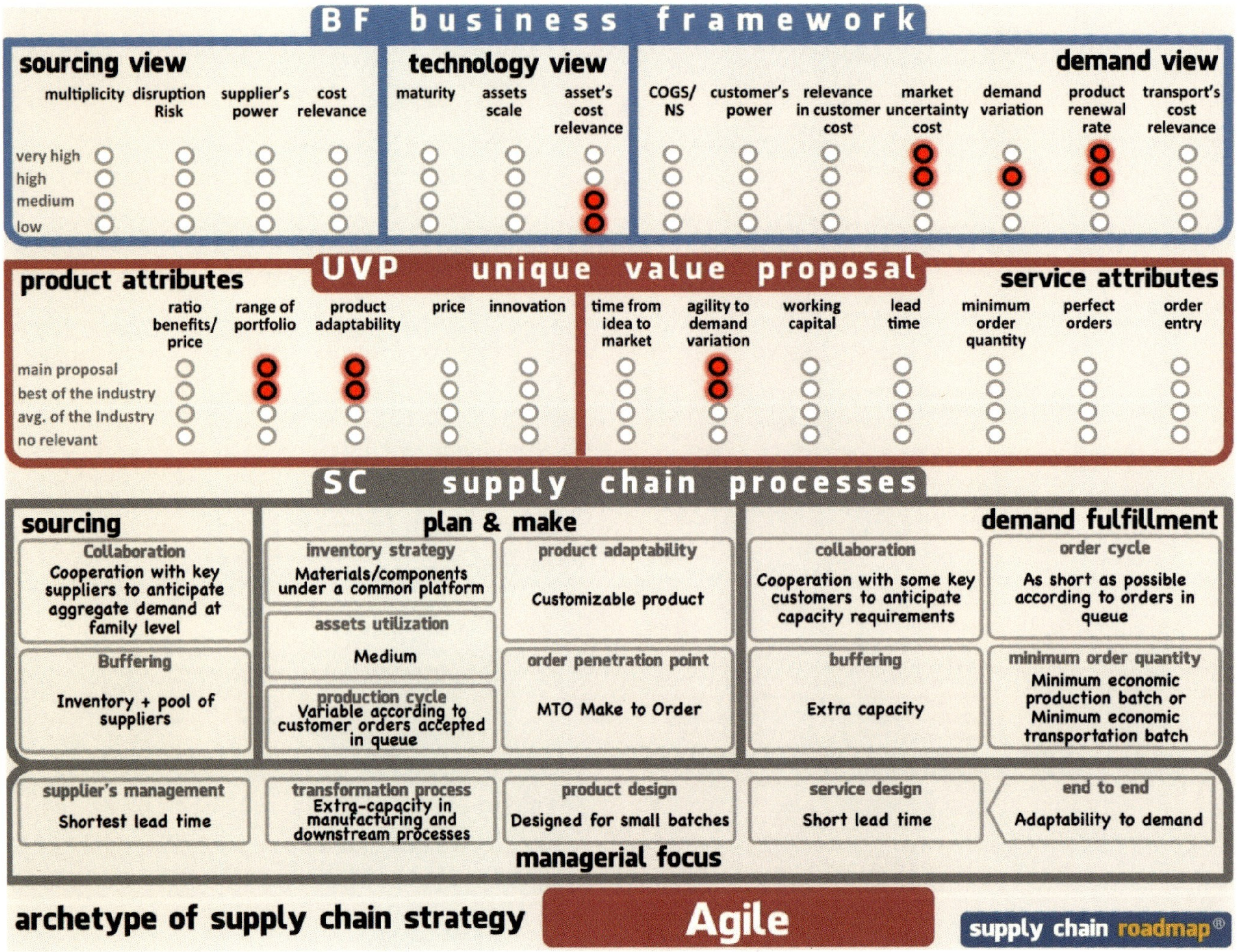

Figure 5.10 Map of the Agile Supply Chain Archetype

The first Archetype of the group of supply chain driven by responsiveness is the "Agile" supply chain, which is characterized by the adaptability to customer's requirements, in terms of both rapid response to variations of demand and product customization.

Figure 5.10 shows the characterization of the factors of the agile Archetype, in which the relevant factors and their characterization are shown.

The main feature of the Business Framework is that demand is unpredictable, which manifests itself in various ways:

Products are customized, which means that products have unique specifications for a customer or group of customers.

Demand volume is highly variable, creating a workload profile with peaks and valleys around average demand.

Lead-time requirement is highly variable, with high variation among customer requests, and in many cases customers request shorter lead-time than those promised by the industry.

Customization entails changing needs of customers, which implies a high product renewal rate.

Combination of both high-demand variation and high-product renewal rate implies a high level of market uncertainty cost.

Customization and unpredictable demand reduces alternative suppliers and substitute products for the customers, thus, customer's power is low, as consequence of that, customers have a loyal behavior, reducing behaviors associated to opportunistic approaches.

Generally, the relevance of assets in the total cost is low or medium, reducing the importance of the asset's utilization in the product price.

The UVP of an agile supply chain is characterized by:

Agility to demand is the most relevant attribute, which balances the high level of demand variation, in order to satisfy: unique product specifications, variable demand volume, and challenging short lead-time.

Price becomes a secondary attribute, allowing the company to offer a higher price than industry's average, or inclusive, offering the highest price of the industry.

Customization obligates the company to have the best approach to product adaptability; consequently, the product range in the portfolio could be nearly unlimited, restricted only by technical considerations.

Customization implies limitations of minimum production batch for each specific product, and consequently, to request by the manufacturer a minimum economic order quantity from customers.

The agile Supply Chain Archetype is useful for companies that manufacture products under unique specifications for each customer. This is typically seen in industries characterized by unpredictable demand. As a result, the main driver of competitiveness is agility: the ability to meet unpredictable demand under unique specifications, in quantities exceeding the customer's forecast, and/or within a shorter lead-time than agreed. The ability to be agile is proportional to the ratio between excess capacity and the average rate of asset usage. In strict terms, there can be no agility without excess capacity.

In the architecture of the supply chain for an agile Archetype, it is important to consider several issues. First, supplier's management should be focused on a collaborative approach in order to have agile sourcing. However, in order to ensure self-agility, a pool of suppliers could be a complimentary countermeasure.

Because customers are oriented to customized products, it results in a unpredictable demand that inhibits the option of a make-to-forecast order penetration point. Consequently, the item is produced after receiving the customer's purchase order, with the purpose of avoiding manufacturing of products for which there is no certainty of future sales. The make-to-order OPP implies full product adaptability in order to produce customized product with the aim of adapting the product to customer needs.

Inventory strategy is focused in maintain enough inventory of components, either raw materials or sourced parts. In order to optimize inventory level, the product portfolio should be oriented to a common platform of components.

Asset utilization is medium in order to maintain enough excess capacity, which is the key component of the agility.

Production cycle and order cycle are variable, according to the length of the queue for processing orders accepted. However, in order to optimize production efficiency, some companies define a production cycle based on an optimal sequence of production, thus reducing time for changeover among SKUs but creating time frames for receiving orders for each group of products.

Demand fulfillment is characterized by a very practical approach, where buffering of demand is supported by excess capacity, and minimum order quantity is related to the minimum economic production batch. In addition to this constraint, it is advisable to use a minimum economic transportation batch (i.e., a full truck load) when relevance of transport cost is high.

Managerial focus should orientate to promote agility, which is supported by three main capabilities: enough excess capacity; products and processes designed to produce the smallest possible batches; and fast transactional processes in order to minimize time used for nonproduction processes—order processing, production scheduling, invoicing and delivery among others—and as consequence of that set short lead-time. Figure 5.11 illustrates the main relationships among factors of the agile Archetype.

Success in this Supply Chain Archetype requires several factors. First, in order to reduce lead-time, materials and components should be under a common platform, which means a group of products built from a set of common components and some specific components for each one. In other words, a set of products shares some key components, and those components should always be available in inventory.

Low-variance customers should be protected by lower prices in order to avoid their defection to efficient competitors. Furthermore, customers with high demand variation should pay higher prices.

Collaborative relationships with key customers are important. They will help suppliers anticipate changes in capacity requirements, both in the short term for scheduling purposes and in the long term for assets investment decisions.

If extra capacity gradually decreases to low levels, the company should invest in additional assets in order to maintain its ability to be agile. If it cannot do so, it should migrate to an efficient or a continuous-flow supply chain in order to adjust its value proposal from agility to efficiency.

Generally, this type of supply chain is employed by manufacturers of intermediary goods that make products for industrial customers according to each customer's specific needs and when industrial customers place a high value on short lead-time. This strategy is useful for industries such as packaging, chemical specialties, and metal machining, among others, where the company's UVP is oriented to offering products on demand under a high service level.

It is important to highlight that inherent in this approach is the temptation to maximize production efficiency, which could generate a high risk of obsolescence, as happened in 2008 to Crocs, the manufacturer of plastic shoes and sandals. In 2006, as part of its supply chain strategy, Crocs opted to have an extra capacity of a million pairs above forecasted sales, allowing them to respond during the selling season with additional orders on best sellers. Unfortunately, poor execution of this policy led to a

114

resounding failure: In a fashion-oriented industry with a high market mediation cost, they began to fill the excess capacity with forecast future sales. Unfortunately, the colors went out of fashion, and this meant an adjustment for obsolescence for more of $60 million.

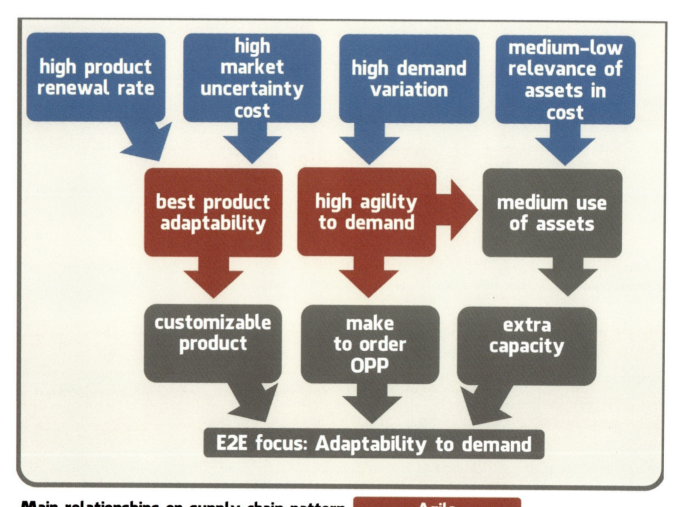

Figure 5.11: Main Relationships of Agile Archetype

The Custom-Configured Supply Chain Archetype

Within the group of supply chain driven by responsiveness, the next Archetype is the "custom-configured" supply chain, which is the combination of an efficient supply chain with an agile supply chain. Figure 5.12 shows the map of supply chain strategy of the Archetype custom configured, in which the relevant factors and their characterization are visible.

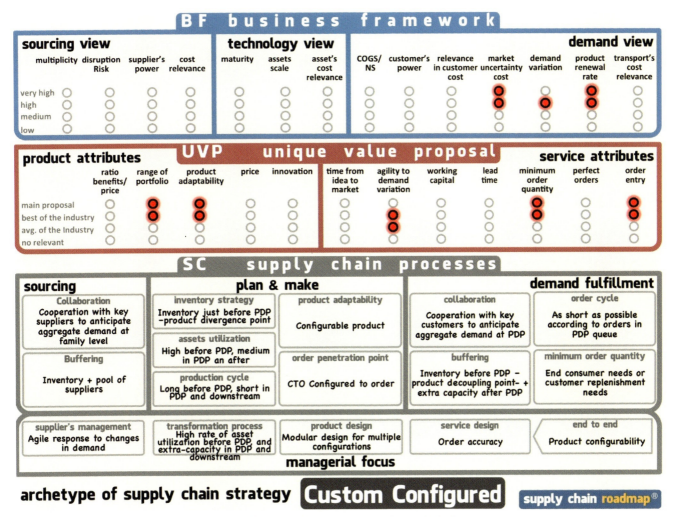

Figure 5.12: Custom Configured Archetype

The Business Framework could have three types of customers:
- No recurrent end-consumers (i.e., individuals) who are consuming high payout and durable goods such as automobiles, computers, etc.
- Recurrent end-consumers, for customized and low-medium payout products, such as tailored garments.
- Industrial consumers oriented to recurrent purchases.

Similar to the agile Supply Chain Archetype, the main feature of the Business Framework is that demand is unpredictable, which manifests itself in several ways:

Products are customized, which means products have unique specifications for a consumer, customer, or group of customers.

Demand volume is highly variable, creating a workload profile with peaks and valleys around the average demand.

Lead-time requirements are highly variable, with high variation among customer requests, and in many cases customers request shorter lead-time than those promised by the industry.

Customization meets the changing needs of customers, which implies a high product renewal rate.

The combination of both high-demand variation and high-product renewal rate implies a high level of market uncertainty cost.

Relevance of assets in the total cost is high before decoupling point and low in and after it. The decoupling point of the transformation process is where the product takes unique specifications for a customer or group of customers. The decoupling point could be located at the same process as the order penetration point, but it is not necessary to be in the same process. In strict terms, where both are located in the same process, inventory is optimized.

In order to ensure optimization of production cost, the assets must be efficient before decoupling point, and they should be agile after it.

The UVP of an agile supply chain is characterized by several factors. Similar to the agile Supply Chain Archetype, agility to demand is the most relevant attribute in this Archetype, offering customers unique product specifications in short lead-time. However, unlike the agile Archetype, efficiency in processes before decoupling point allows the company to maintain a competitive price.

Customization requires a deep approach around product adaptability; consequently, the range of the company's portfolio could be very high, limited only by the allowed combination of components and features into the same product.

A unit minimum quantity order is an important requirement in order to enhance the supply chain's scope to end-consumers.

Figure 5.13 shows the main relationships among the factors of the custom configured Archetype.

The custom-configured Supply Chain Archetype is characterized by a high degree of relevance of the cost of assets to the total cost and (potentially unlimited) multiple configurations of the finished product under a unique platform in which products share some materials and/or parts. Competitive positioning is founded on offering a unique configuration of the finished product according to the end consumer's needs. Unlike in an agile supply chain, where the product can be customized to meet virtually any customer requirement—*limited only by technical constraints*—in this supply chain, the product is configurable within a limited combination of product specifications, usually by combining parts into a set or assembly.

Usually, product configuration is accomplished during an assembly process, where some of the parts are mounted or assembled according to individual customers' requirements. However, product configuration may be done in other types of processes, such as mixing, packaging, and printing, among others. As a general rule, the processes before product configuration are lengthier than the configuration itself and the downstream processes.

In the architecture of the supply chain for a custom-configured Supply Chain Archetype, it is important to consider several factors. First, supplier's management should be focused on a collaborative approach in order to have agile sourcing. However, in order to ensure agility, a pool of suppliers could be a complimentary countermeasure.

Because customers are oriented to customized products, demand results in a unpredictable pattern which inhibit the option of a make to forecast order penetration point. Consequently, the use of a configured to order OPP allows assembling or configuring the product after receiving the customer's purchase order, with the purpose of producing products for which there is a complete certainty of sale. It means, before decoupling point, the OPP is a make to forecast, and, after decoupling point, the OPP it is likely to make to order, but in strictly terms, the OPP for the Custom Configured Archetype should be named configured to order. The configured to order OPP implies high product adaptability in order to assemble customized product with the aim to adapting product to meet customer needs.

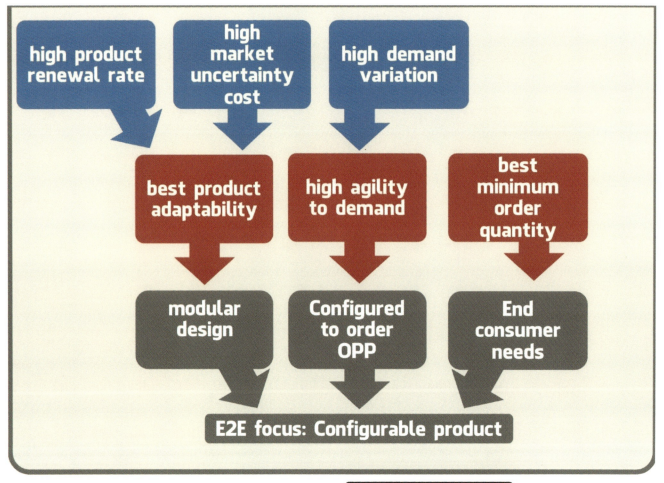

Figure 5.13: Main Relationships in Custom Configured Archetype

Inventory strategy is focused on maintaining enough inventory of manufactured components and/or semi-finished products; in order to optimize inventory level, product portfolio should oriented to a common platform of components and/or semi-finished products.

Asset utilization is medium in and after decoupling point in order to maintain enough excess capacity, which is the key component of the agility. Before decoupling point, asset utilization is high in order to allocate fixed costs in the highest number of produced units.

Demand fulfillment is characterized by a very practical approach, with buffering supported by enough inventory of components and excess capacity in and after decoupling point.

Minimum order quantity is defined as: (1) A unit for products produced under discrete manufacturing like assembled products (e.g. computers, automobiles, and industrial equipment); and, (2) A minimum economic production batch for products produced under continuous production.

Managerial focus should orientate to promote product configurability, which is supported by four main capabilities:

- Modularity of components, which are designed under a same platform, allowing interchangeability.
- Products and processes designed to produce the smallest possible production batches (in the case of process production) and/or oriented to discrete production (i.e., production by units).
- Accurate and friendly order entry in order to ensure understanding of customer's specifications and to ensure the flow of this information along the configuration process.
- Fast transactional processes in order to minimize time used for nonproduction processes: order processing, production scheduling, invoicing, and delivery among others and, consequently, set short lead-time.

Success in this Supply Chain Archetype requires several factors. First, the order-entry system should be detailed and accurate as well user-friendly to ensure, respectively, a clear understanding of customer requirements and ease of use from the customer's perspective.

Processes before decoupling point should be managed under the criteria of an efficient or a continuous-flow supply chain, according to the characteristics of the demand profile. Configuration and downstream processes should be managed under the criteria of an agile supply chain.

Because of the nearly unlimited number of possible finished products resulting from multiple combinations of parts or materials, it is practically impossible to make an accurate forecast of finished product. However, before the decoupling point, components should be produced under a make-to-forecast or make-to-stock OPP.

Manufacturers should maximize the number of possible configurations for a product platform and, in turn, minimize the materials and/or parts used for that product platform. This is the key factor in reducing complexity in this type of supply chain. It is important to maximize the number of possible product's configurations with the minimum number of components on inventory.

To prevent the order cycle from becoming longer, it is necessary to ensure the full availability of materials and/or parts before the configuration process. The most popular product configurations should be available in of finished-goods inventory, managed under an efficient or a continuous-flow Supply Chain Archetype.

Examples of where this supply chain makes sense include the assembly of personalized products, such as computers and vehicles, and the paper manufacturing industry, where the decoupling point occurs after the manufacture of the big rolls and the products are customized in the cutting and packaging process. In the service sector, some fast food restaurants apply this Supply Chain Archetype.

Toyota, one of the most recognized supply chains around the world, is perhaps the paradigm in best practice around product customization. Toyota created the Toyota Production System, often called Lean Manufacturing and often misinterpreted as a supply chain oriented to efficiency. Really, Toyota supply chain is a custom-configured Supply Chain Archetype, but with a big improvement against the typical custom-configured supply chain, because they reach high levels of efficiency through the end-to-end process. Toyota has evolved his supply chain, and a recent development was the supply chain for the Scion model. The Toyota Scion was launched in the United States in 2003 as a car aimed at young people who desired to have a unique and exclusive car; it was probably the first no luxury vehicle allowing customization. The customer can choose from more than 40 accessories, and can select color, transmission, sound, and rims. Unlike luxury cars, customization takes place in the port of destination or into the facilities of the dealer, where modular components are assembled to the vehicle. This approach allows Toyota to maximize production efficiency in the factory, where relevance of assets in total cost is higher.

The Flexible Supply Chain

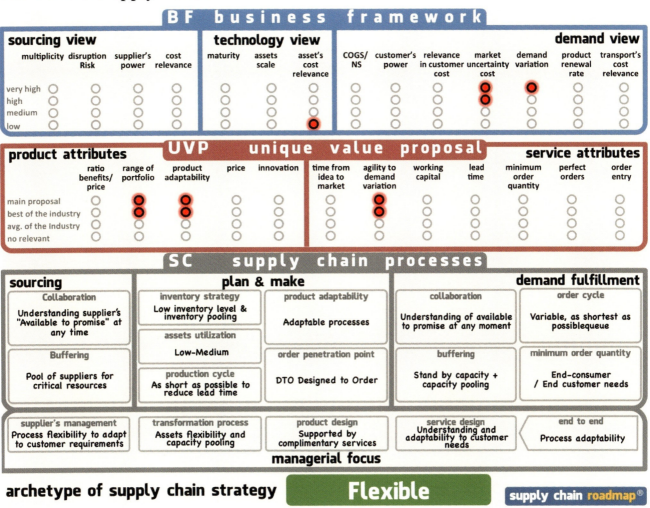

Figure 5.14: Flexible Archetype

A Flexible supply chain is the highest level of adaptability to customer's needs. In this Archetype, both the product and the productive processes have a high degree of flexibility in order to create an unique solution for an specific customer's need. Figure 5.14 shows the map of supply chain strategy of the Archetype flexible, in which the relevant factors and their characterization are shown.

The Business Framework of the sixth Supply Chain Archetype, flexible, is characterized by several factors. The main difference with the agile and custom-configured Supply Chain Archetypes is in the demand pattern, which is under extreme conditions, thus manifests in several ways:

- Products are customized at the highest level, which means products are unique for each customer order, and, generally, customers are non recurrent.
- Customization implies not only unique product specifications, but also as modifications of production processes in order to produce the product.
- Demand volume is highly variable, creating a workload profile with long periods of low or without demand and very short periods of demand peaks.
- Lead-time requirements are highly demanding; customers require a very fast solution of their needs.
- Customization entails specific and unique needs of customers, which implies a high product renewal rate.
- Combination of both high-demand variation and high-product renewal rate implies the highest level of market uncertainty cost.
- Relevance of assets in the total cost is low.

The UVP of a flexible supply chain is characterized by several factors. First, similar to agile and custom-configured Supply Chain Archetypes, agility to demand is the most relevant attribute in both product customization and shorter lead-time. Customization requires the highest approach to product adaptability. Consequently, the range of portfolio could be infinite, limited only by the technical restrictions of the adaptability of the production processes.

A unit minimum quantity order is an important requirement in order to enhance the supply chain's scope to provide the solutions required by each customer.

Due to the unique and exclusive of the solution for each customer, price is not a relevant attribute for the customer.

The flexible Supply Chain Archetype is suited to companies that must meet unexpected demand and therefore are faced with high demand peaks and long periods of low workload. This Supply Chain Archetype is characterized by adaptability, which is the capability to reconfigure internal processes in order to solve a customer's specific need. This Archetype typically is used by service companies, which are focused on addressing unexpected situations and emergencies. Due to the nature of such events, customers appreciate not only the supplier's speed of response, but also its ability to tailor solutions to their needs. Consequently, price becomes irrelevant to the customer.

On the other hand in the perspective of Supply Chain Processes, it is important to consider several characteristic factors of the flexible Supply Chain Archetype:

Supplier's management should be focused on the management of a pool of suppliers that share in a permanent way their available-to-promise capacity at any moment. It allows management to focus the requirements on those suppliers with enough capacity, which increases responsiveness.

Product adaptability is at the highest level. It implies a design-to-order OPP; consequently, both product and transformation processes are adapted to each customer order.

Inventory strategy is focused on maintaining a low level of inventory of components and a pooling of components shared with competitors and customers.

Assets utilization is low. Therefore, instead of having a unique or few units of high throughput equipment, it is recommended to have many units of low throughput equipment, which enhances flexibility.

Demand fulfillment is characterized by an approach oriented to understanding and satisfying customer needs. Buffering is supported by capacity on stand by and pooling of capacity with competitors.

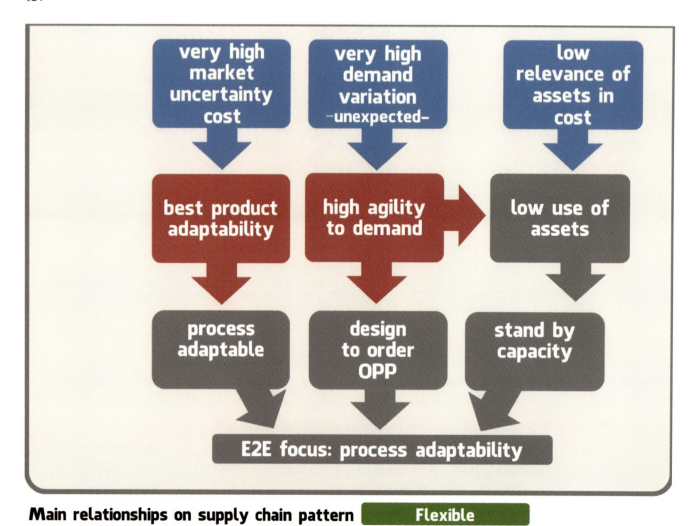

Figure 5.15: Main Relationships in Flexible Supply Chain Archetype

Managerial focus should orientate to promote adaptability, which is supported by five main capabilities: stand-by capacity of critical resources; many low-throughput assets; technical strengths in process and product engineering; quick response from order entry to product-process design; and a process flow that is designed to be quickly reconfigurable.

Main relationships among factors of the flexible Archetype are shown in the Figure 5.15.

Success in the flexible Supply Chain Archetype requires several factors. First, companies should keep critical resources, such as pumps for companies orientated to flood recovery or metal machining equipment for spare parts manufacturing, available on stand by. This may require pooling of such resources, including with those of competitors, because these companies are oriented to addressing unexpected situations in which capacity could be easily overpassed and it is not economical feasible to have infinite capacity.

Strong collaborative relationships with key suppliers are necessary in order to understand at every moment their current available-to-promise inventory and capacity.

Adaptability is based on having many resources of low-to-medium capacity instead of a few resources of high capacity.

A well-designed order-entry process is critical in order to ensure a proper understanding of the customer's situation and requirements.

A typical example of this type of supply chain can be found in companies that provide metalworking and machining services for the manufacture of spare parts for industrial customers. They require a fast response and sufficient capacity to develop unique parts by combining successive processes, such as turning, reaming, and welding, in a configuration adapted to a specific situation.

Another example of this Supply Chain Archetype can be found companies oriented to solve unexpected situations such as the recovery of assets. The Revival Company, which is based in the United Kingdom and serves recovery of disasters such as fire, flood, and fluid spills, provides the specific design of the solution together with the insurance company, the adjuster, and the owner. Their availability promise is 24 hours 7 days a week and a response time of less than an hour. In addition to that, they have a proprietary technology for fast drying and the biggest quantity of drying machines in Europe. All the above—design of personalized solutions, quick response, and stand-by capacity—meets the main characteristics of a flexible Supply Chain Archetype.

Comparison of Supply Chains Oriented to Responsiveness

Figure 5.16 shows a comparison among the three Supply Chain Archetypes oriented to responsiveness, in which the main factors of the three perspectives and the typical qualification for each Archetype are shown.

		Custom Configured	Agile	Flexible
Business Framework	Asset's cost relevance	High - Very High before Product Divergence Point	Low - Medium	Low
	Market uncertainty cost	High - Very High	High - Very High	High - Very High
	Demand Variation	High	High	Very High
Unique Value Proposal	Price	Whatever	Whatever	No relevant, usually very expensive
	Agility to demand	Average or best	Average or best	Average or Best
	Main Value Proposal	Multiple configurations for customization	Agile and adaptable to demand	Customizable Solutions
Supply Chain Processes	Product Adaptability	Configurable Product	Customizable Product	Adaptable processes
	Inventory Strategy	Inventory just before PDP - product divergence point	Materials/components under a common platform	Low inventory level & inventory pooling
	Asset's utilization	High before PDP, medium in PDP an after	Medium	Low - Medium
	Order Penetration Point	Configurable to Order	Make to Order	Designed to Order
	Demand buffering	Inventory before PDP + extra capacity after PDP	Extra Capacity	Stand by capacity + capacity pooling
	End to End Managerial Focus	Product Configurability	Adaptability to demand	Process Adaptability

Figure 5.16: Comparison of Supply Chain Archetypes oriented to responsiveness

These Archetypes face high levels of demand variation and market uncertainty cost and, consequently, the requirement of a high level of product adaptability compared against the supply chains oriented to efficiency. The main distinctions among these Archetypes are caused by the differences on the degree of product adaptability, which is lower on the Custom Configured Archetype. In this Archetype, the product divergence point is located in the middle of the transformation process; usually a finishing process (e.g., packing, mixing, cutting, printing or assembly among others) is where product is configured according to customer's requirements. Customization is limited by the finishing options or configurations available (called "configurable to order"). Therefore, the inventory is in parts, components, or semi-finished products located before being processed in the finishing process.

On the other hand, the Agile Archetype has the product divergence point located at the beginning of the transformation process. The customers define product specifications before any product processing. In this case, customization is limited by the technical restrictions of the transformation processes, and the inventory is in raw materials or purchased components located before processing.

Finally, the Flexible Archetype has the product divergence point located at the stage of solution design, meaning the solution is designed according to the specific need of the customer, and the transformation processes are highly flexible in order to allow the adaptability to each designed solution.

Chapter 06
Feasibility Matrix

The way to select the proper supply chain archetype for your business

Tool 4: Feasibility Matrix

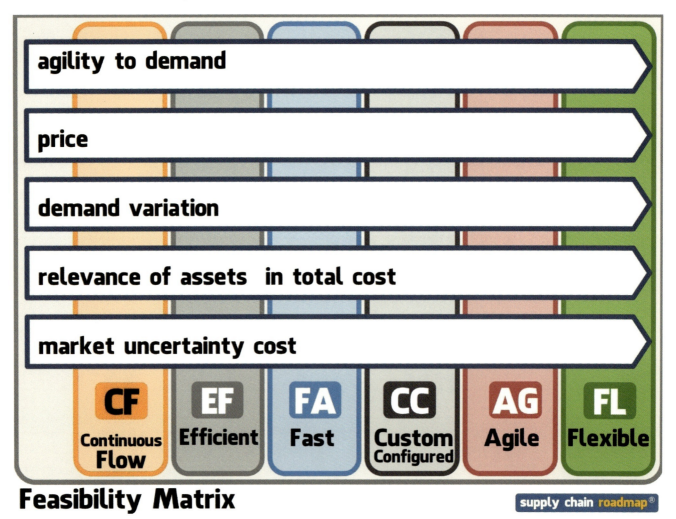

Figure 6.1: Relationships on the Feasibility Matrix

The fourth tool is the Feasibility Matrix, which allows for the selection of the proper Supply Chain Archetype for the organization under assessment; in order to compare the supply chain under evaluation with the proper Archetype, and consequently to found the gaps between them.

The Feasibility Matrix has in the vertical axis, two attributes of the Unique Value Proposal, and, three factors of the Business Framework:
- Agility to demand,
- Price,
- Demand variation,
- Relevance of assets in total cost
- Market uncertainty cost,

And, the Feasibility Matrix has in the horizontal axis the six Supply Chain Archetypes:
- Efficient,
- Fast,
- Continuous Flow,
- Agile,
- Custom Configured,
- Flexible.

In the intersection among factors and Archetypes appears the qualification of each factor / attribute, which became in the input data. Therefore, for each combination of factors, there is a recommended Archetype, as is presented in Figure 6.2.

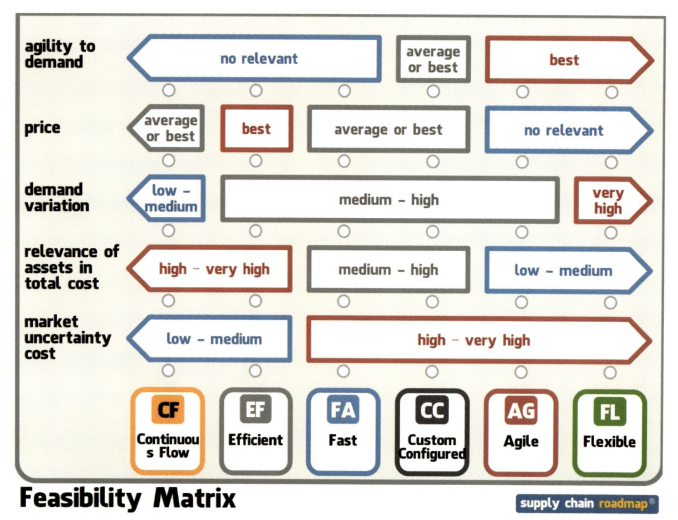

Figure 6.2: Feasibility Matrix

SECTION 3: Applying the Method

Understanding the concepts and tools of the Supply Chain Roadmap can lead to better comprehension of the steps to use the supply chain roadmap method in the analysis of a supply chain.

The 4-Step Method is a organized and schematic approach to apply the Supply Chain Roadmap method in the analysis of an organization's supply chain.

Chapter 07
4-Step Method

The guide to apply Supply Chain Roadmap

Supply Chain Roadmap's Four-Step Method

The four-step method (Figure 7.1) provides a step-by-step guide for analyzing a real supply chain using the four tools of the Supply Chain Roadmap.

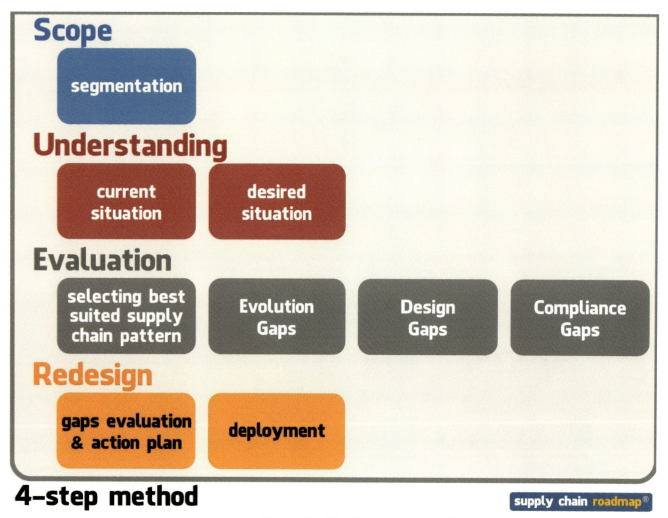

Figure 7.1: The Four-step Method

Before applying the four-step method, it is necessary to assemble an assessment team, which should be composed of people from the top-level functions of marketing, sales, supply chain, operations, and finance. In addition, it is important to have people from other levels with strong knowledge of Supply Chain Processes and customer behavior.

An experienced executive of the company under assessment can lead the assessment, but for best results is recommended that the organization hire a facilitator with experience in conducting assessments of strategic planning or supply chain improvement.

Step 1: Scope

Organizations tend to want their supply chains to have simultaneous capabilities: efficient, fast, agile, and flexible, among others. However, each of these capabilities requires different skills, and in the majority of cases, these skill sets are incompatible within the same supply chain. It is possible, though, to develop several parallel supply chains within a single organization, each focused on a defined market segment with a responsiveness level and a cost structure that are appropriate to the segment it serves. This is precisely the purpose of the first step: Understand which supply chains operate within the organization, segment the scope of each of them, and focus the analysis under Supply Chain Roadmap method.

There are three general rules for segmenting the supply chains, as shown in Figure 7.2:

Minimize: The supply chain of the organization must be segmented into the minimum number of supply chains, in order to avoid the complexity of a lot of supply chains, which could be inoperable.

Uniqueness: Every segment should have a Unique Value Proposal, which should be suitable for all the products or customers classified in them, in order to avoid broad and undefined UVPs, as a result of segments combining a mixture of multiple and dissimilar members.

Simplicity: Use one criterion of segmentation; in exceptional cases, use the combination of two criteria of segmentation, aiming to avoid the complexity of a matrix criteria.

The first rule of segmentation promotes the minimization of supply chains. The second rule avoids the temptation to group under a same segment those supply chains with dissimilar characteristics.

The third rule aims to avoid complexity on the segmentation. The compliance of these rules allows optimizing the segmentation of the supply chains into the organization.

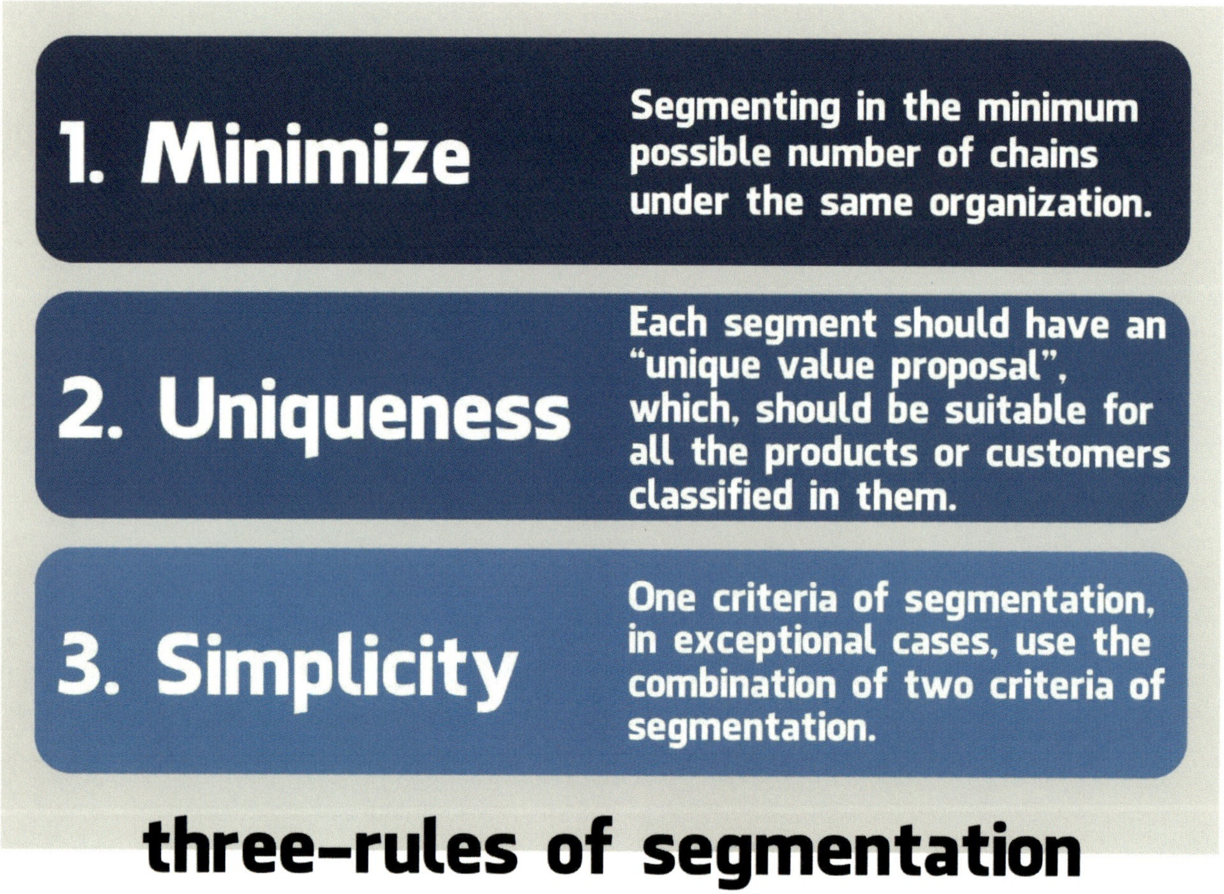

1. Minimize — Segmenting in the minimum possible number of chains under the same organization.

2. Uniqueness — Each segment should have an "unique value proposal", which, should be suitable for all the products or customers classified in them.

3. Simplicity — One criteria of segmentation, in exceptional cases, use the combination of two criteria of segmentation.

three-rules of segmentation

Figure 7.2: Rules for Segmentation

In order to ensure compliance of the three rules of segmentation, it is necessary to determine the right criterion to segment the supply chains; segmentation criteria could be classified according to several approaches, which are based on customers or products:

Customer behavior. Customers are classified according to their willingness to develop long-term relationships. Customer behavior could be classified as:

Opportunistic: Customers who are willing to do business with whomever has the best price at the moment.

Collaborative: Customers with a stable demand pattern, who are willing to create long-term relationships and are looking for the development of synergies between both.

No recurrent: Customers with whom transactions are conducted in batches with a long time gap between them; however, this is not the result of an opportunistic behavior. Instead, discontinuity of transactions is the result of sporadic need of the products.

Unsteady: Customers with an unsteady demand pattern who are willing to have a partner prepared to support changing behavior.

Product adaptability. This classification is based on the adaptability of the products to customer needs: standardized product, changing product, configurable product, customizable product, customizable solution.

Product length of life. This classification is based on products denoted according to their relative rate of renewal and/or market uncertainty cost. For example, in apparel, the supply chain could be segmented in two: "classic products" such as basic colors in polo shirts, and "trendy products" such as print shirts with licensed characters.

Demand variation. This classification is based on products or customers, which are arranged according to their relative variance of demand. A practical rule is to classify them based on variance against forecast. Magnitude of variance changes across industries and markets. As a result, ranges should be defined for each specific case based on the understanding of their particular behavior. Despite this criteria could be useful for products and customers, it is not recommendable to use for customers; in this case is a better approach to segment based on customer behavior.

Sales volume. This classification is based on products or customers, according to their relative volume of sales. A practical rule is to classify them based on Pareto's principle, grouping products or customers that make 80% of the sales volume.

Distribution channel. This classification is based on products and probably is one of the most used criterion for segmenting supply chains. This criterion supposes that customers in the same distribution channel have strong similarities among them. Customers are classified as either wholesalers, distributors, small groceries, convenience, or superstores, etc.

Product profitability. In this category, products are classified as either high-margin or low-margin products. The magnitude of profitability changes across industries and markets, and, as a result, ranges should be defined for each specific case based on the understanding of their particular behavior.

Relevance of assets in total cost. This classification is based on the relative importance of the fixed cost of assets in the total cost of products. This criterion is useful when a company manufactures products in exclusive assets and when assets have fixed cost magnitude and/or production scales at opposite ends.

Length of sourcing. This classification is based on the clustering of products according to their relative length of sourcing, since components ordering until finished product is available for dispatching. Products are classified according to which have imported components and which are 100% manufactured with local components.

After segmentation is done, the next step is "Understanding", which allows to characterize each of the supply chains resulting of the segmentation.

Step 2: Understanding

After supply chains are segmented, it is necessary to understand each of the segmented supply chains under the three perspectives of the Map: *Business Framework, Unique Value Proposal, and Supply Chain Processes*. In other words, Understanding is the realization of conversations within the team, in order to allow the proper description and characterization into the Map of Supply Chain Strategy (Tool 1) of each of the supply chains under assessment.

Understanding should be done according to two scenarios: the first focused on the understanding of the current status of the supply chain, and the second based on the understanding of a future or desired situation. Figure 7.3 describes the phases of this step.

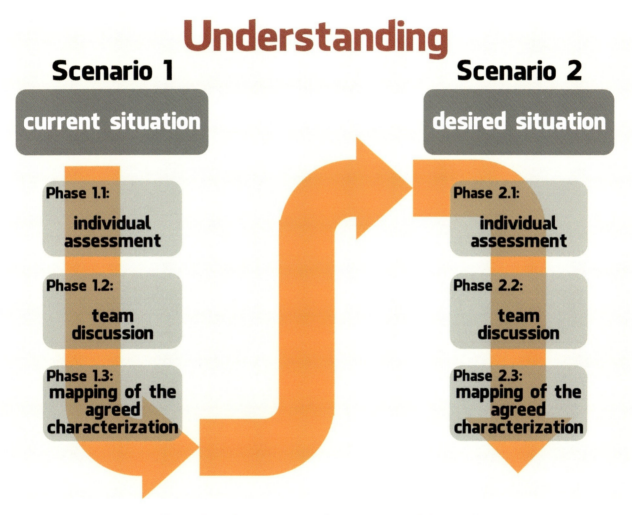

Figure 7.3: Phases for Describing Current and Future Situations

The session for doing the second step (Understanding) should be done in three phases for each scenario: an individual evaluation performed by each of the people conforming the assessment team; a team discussion, aimed at understanding several points of view of the participants and reaching a final consensus of the understanding of the three perspectives of the map for each scenario (current and future); and, finally, the description of what was agreed on the map -*Tool 1*-, as is shown in Figure 7.4.

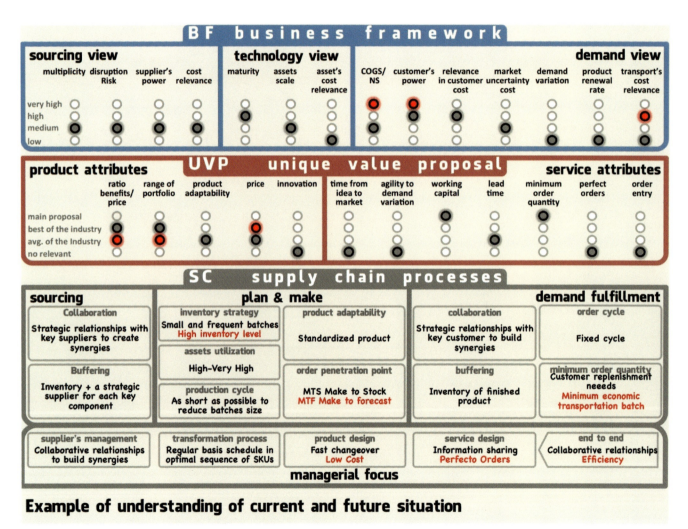

Figure 7.4: Current and Future Situations in a Single Map

A good practice is to use the same map for evaluating both situations, using a different color pencil for the future situation and avoiding to write description of the future situation when it remains equal to the current situation. This allows for a visual understanding of both situations and their gaps, as shown in Figure 7.4, where the current situation is shown in text on black and circles on gray, and the future situation is shown in circles and text on red.

It is important to avoid common pitfalls when examining the current situation:

Misunderstanding. Complete understanding of the Supply Chain Roadmap method requires leveling of the knowledge and unification of meaning of concepts, whereby is recommendable to prepare a workshop -for all of the people conforming the assessment team- about concepts explained in chapters 1 to 6.

Enhance company's performance. When companies are under an evaluation tends to overestimate the real performance. In order to avoid this behavior, it is useful that the leader of the assessment realize interviews with customers aiming to have a real benchmark against relevant competitors. Interviews should be focused on evaluating the company's performance against relevant competitors under the factors of the Unique Value Proposal.

Lack of understanding of industry. For a real understanding of Business Framework, it would be useful to have results of market research and data of demand and supply for both customers and suppliers, in order to have a proper understanding of the Business Framework based on facts, more than in assumptions.

Poor segmentation. Where a lack of consensus in the qualification of some factors is present, it is advisable to review the properness of the segmentation in order to verify if there are grouped customers or products with dissimilar behaviors.

Changing time frame. People involved in the analysis tend to put in the current time frame, behaviors, or situations that actually are not happening but are likely to occur. This behaviors or situations should be isolated, and define the appropriate future scenario to consider them..

Passing to the Future situation it is recommendable to frame the scenario under analysis, according to one of the following approaches:

Improvement of competitive positioning. In this scenario, the Business Framework is the same for both situations—current and future—and the future situation is focused on the determination of the changes of the UVP and Supply Chain Processes.

Evaluation of "what if?" situations. In this scenario, the main purpose is to anticipate future changes in the industry and to evaluate changes in the Business Framework, such as higher transportation cost, a higher power of customers against the industry by the entry of a new competitor, changes in technology, etc., and their consequences on the UVP and the Supply Chain Processes.

Understanding allows to characterize the organization's supply chain under the Map. After Understanding is done, the next step is "Evaluation", which allows to determine the gaps between the supply chain under analysis and the referrals (10 Common-Patterns, Archetypes, and Future Situation).

Step 3: Evaluation

After supply chains are understood, it is necessary to evaluate each of the segmented supply chains under the three main referrals:

Future situation
Best-suited Supply Chain Archetype
10-Common-Patterns

The differences found when evaluating the supply chain under analysis can be of two types:

Sectorial change. This refers to differences in the Business Framework between the current and desired situations. These are difficult to modify because they are a consequence of the changes and evolution of the industrial sector –sectorial changes-. When company under assessment is a leader in the industrial sector, the company could lead some changes in the Business Framework of the industrial sector, like, introduction of new technologies, collaborative approach with customers in order to reduce demand variation, introduction of changes in the behaviors of customers, etc.

Differences in factors of the Business Framework between the supply chain under analysis and the Supply Chain Archetype are not considered as a sectorial change, but should be analyzed in order to verify relevance and properness of the Supply Chain Archetype selected.

Gap, is a divergence between the supply chain under analysis and the referrals. Depending on the referral, the gap may be one of three types:

- **Design** —a difference between the supply chain under analysis and the Supply Chain Archetype in a factor of the internal perspectives -*Unique Value Proposal and Supply Chain Processes*-.
- **Evolution**—a difference between the current situation and the future situation of the supply chain under analysis in a factor of the internal perspectives -*Unique Value Proposal and Supply Chain Processes*-.
- **Compliance**—When the Common Pattern is present in the supply chain under analysis -*the factors of the Business Framework and the attributes of the Common Pattern are equal for both: supply chain under analysis and Common Pattern*-, and, a factor of the supply chain process is different from the recommended guidelines defined for the Common Pattern under analysis.

Selecting the Best Suited Supply Chain Archetype

Before starting evaluation of gaps, the assessment team must determine which Supply Chain Archetype is best suited to the organization by comparing the supply chain under analysis. To do so, it is necessary to use Tool 4: Feasibility Matrix.

Based on The Map of the current situation—*use Map of the future situation in cases where it has high and soon probability of occurrence*—should be qualified the factors of the Feasibility Matrix:

- Mark the circles below the proper qualification for each factor.
- Count the marked circles for each Supply Chain Archetype.
- Select the Supply Chain Archetype with the highest number of marked circles.

In the case of the Figure 7.5, there are five coincidences for the efficient supply chain, which should be the referral –Best Suited Supply Chain Archetype- for the gap analysis.

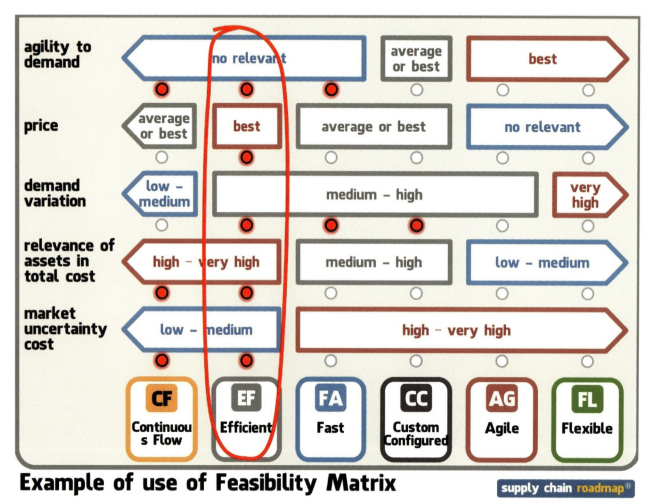

Figure 7.5: Example of Use of Feasibility Matrix in a Case of a Single Dominant Supply Chain

In some cases, two dominant supply chains could exist with the same number of coincidences. In order to define which one is best suited to the organization, the Archetype that has coincidence in the attributes of agility to demand and price should be selected. If the coincidence persists, it should be solved based on the coincidence with the market uncertainty cost.

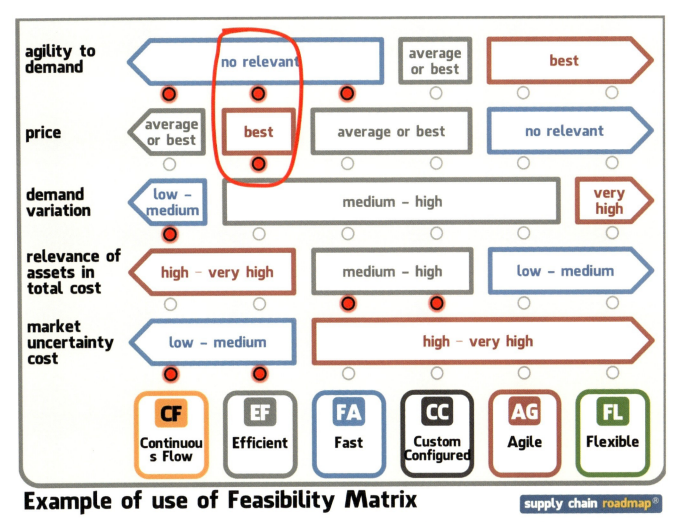

Figure 7.6: Using Feasibility Matrix in a Case of Two Dominant Supply Chains

In the case of Figure 7.6 there are two dominant supply chains –*Both, Continuous Flow and Efficient Archetypes have three coincidences, marked by red circles, in the five factors*-, which, according to the criteria previously defined is solved in favor of the efficient supply chain –*which became in the Archetype for this case*-, because this has coincidence on both factors agility to demand and price, as is highlighted by the red line around the qualifications for the efficient Archetype.

Evolution Gaps

Evolution gaps were defined as "a difference between the current situation and the future situation of the supply chain under analysis in a factor of the internal perspectives -*Unique Value Proposal and Supply Chain Processes*".

Evolution gaps are useful for understanding the changes in the Business Framework—i.e., changes on the industrial sector—that will be faced by the organization in the near future. Consequently, evolution gaps are helpful in identifying the evolution of the organization's UVP and its impact on the Supply Chain Processes, in order to anticipate the actions required to develop a future supply chain.

Gaps between current and desired situations should be analyzed using a map where both scenarios and the differences between them are clearly visible. Figure 7.7 shows:

- The future situation is shown in text on red color, and circles highlighted in red color
- A current situation in text on black letters and circles highlighted in gray color
- When factors of both scenarios are equal, there are not description of the future situation
- Changes on the industrial sector between both scenarios are highlighted by a line in blue
- Green line highlights gaps between current and future situations of the Unique Value Proposal and Supply Chain Processes.

In this example, the Business Framework is moving to a higher ratio COGS/NS, transport cost relevance, and customer's power. Consequently, UVP moves to a higher importance of price, and the supply chain factors evolve from continuous flow to an efficient focused supply chain.

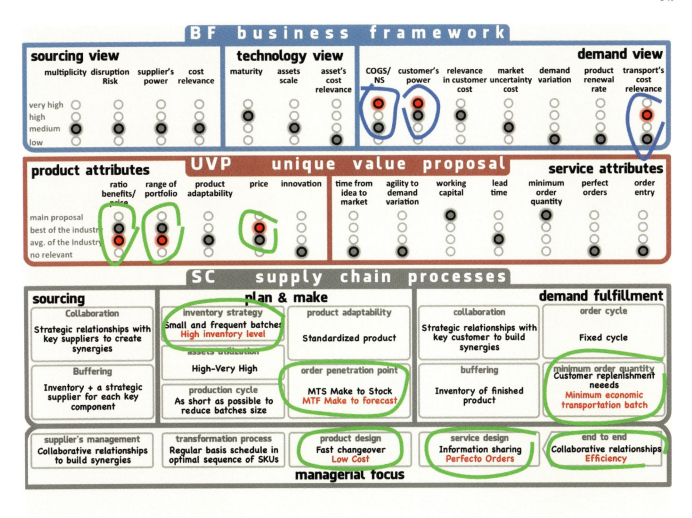

Figure 7.7: Example of a Map After Analysis of Evolution Gaps

Design Gaps

As was explained previously, a Design Gap is a difference in a factor of the internal perspectives -*Unique Value Proposal and Supply Chain Processes*-, between the supply chain under analysis and the best Supply Chain Archetype.

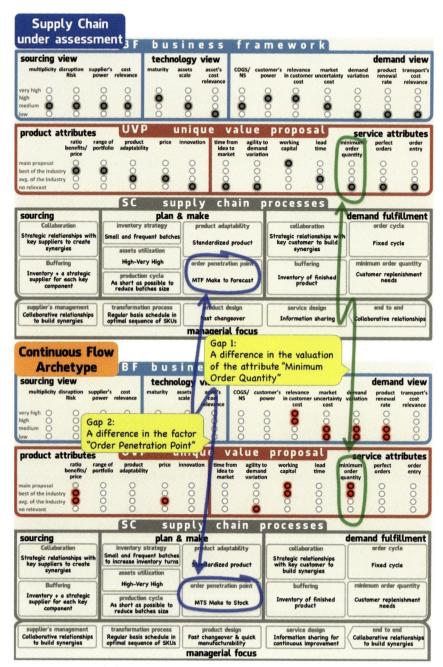

Figure 7.8: Example of Analysis of Design Gaps

Design gaps allow for the understanding of the differences between the supply chain under assessment and the best-suited Archetype, which constitutes in a prototype that could be copied, adapted, or emulated by the supply chain under assessment. The main purpose of the design gaps is to visualize the differences between the supply chain under analysis and the best practice represented in the Archetype, as will be explained further, a gap is not necessarily a wrong practice.

Design gaps are visualized under a comparison of both maps: map of the supply chain under assessment and map of the best-suited Supply Chain Archetype.

In Figure 7.8, the supply chain under assessment is compared against the continuous flow Archetype. Such comparison reveals two gaps: the first related to minimum order quantity policy, and the second related to the order penetration point.

Compliance Gaps

As was defined previously, a Compliance gaps is the failure to observe of the recommendations of some of the 10-Common-Patterns.

Compliance gaps is aimed at verifying compliance of the rules and recommended guidelines of the Common Patterns, which must be ensured in order to avoid basic mistakes because they can cause major misalignments between supply chain and business strategy.

Compliance gaps are visualized under a comparison of both maps: map of the supply chain under assessment and map of each of the ten Common Patterns.

In Figure 7.9, the supply chain under assessment is compared against Common Pattern 1, "Industries in a High Challenging Sourcing," which reveals that the pattern is not present in the case under analysis; therefore, no gap is present.

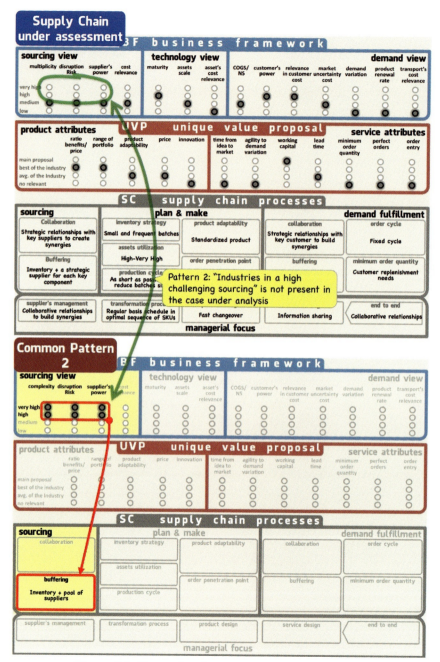

Figure 7.9: Example of Analysis of Common Patterns Gaps

Evaluation step allows to determine the gaps between the supply chain under analysis and the referrals (10 Common-Patterns, Archetypes, and Future Situation); the final step is the Redesign & Deployment, which allows to define the action plan to close the gaps.

Step 4: Redesign & Deployment

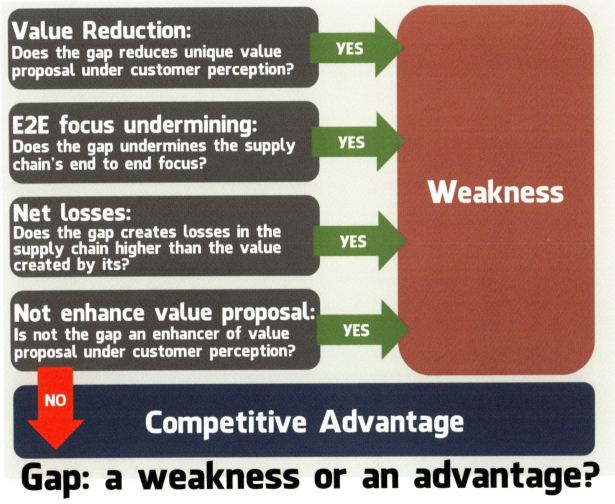

Figure 7.10: Criteria for Analyzing a Gap

The redesign and deployment step aims for the evaluation and closing of gaps, as is known, a gap reflects a difference against a referral, therefore, is necessary to evaluate the nature of the gap, in order to determine whether this is a competitive advantage or a weakness.

For qualifying a gap as a weakness, it is recommended to verify the compliance of at least one of the following criteria:

- Does the gap reduce the UVP as relates to customer perception?
- Does the gap undermine the supply chain's end-to-end focus?
- Does the gap create losses in the supply chain higher than the value created by it?
- For qualifying a gap as a competitive advantage, it is recommend that the organization verify compliance by answering the questions above to determine whether the gap is the enhancer of an attribute and whether this attribute is positively valued under customer perception. These criteria are shown in Figure 7.10.

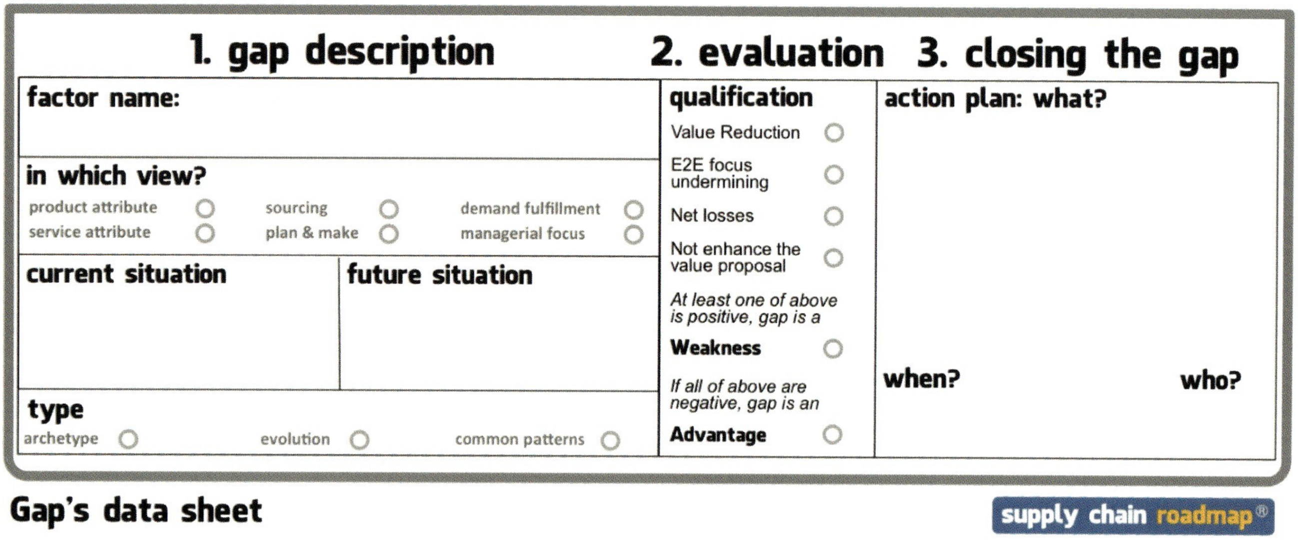

Figure 7.11: Data Sheet for Gap Analysis

In order to evaluate gap relevance, the gap data sheet is used (see Figure 7.11). The gap data sheet allows the organization to describe, evaluate, and define the action plan to close any gaps. Gaps could be eliminated by a change in the design of the supply chain strategy or by changing individual factors and/or a set of factors.

After each gap is visualized, information about each gap should be filled in on the gap's data sheet. (In Figure 7.7, there are nine gaps). This allows for the examination of all the information about the gap and the action plan for eliminating any gaps; otherwise, when the gap is an advantage, the reason for this is explained, as is shown in Figure 7.12.

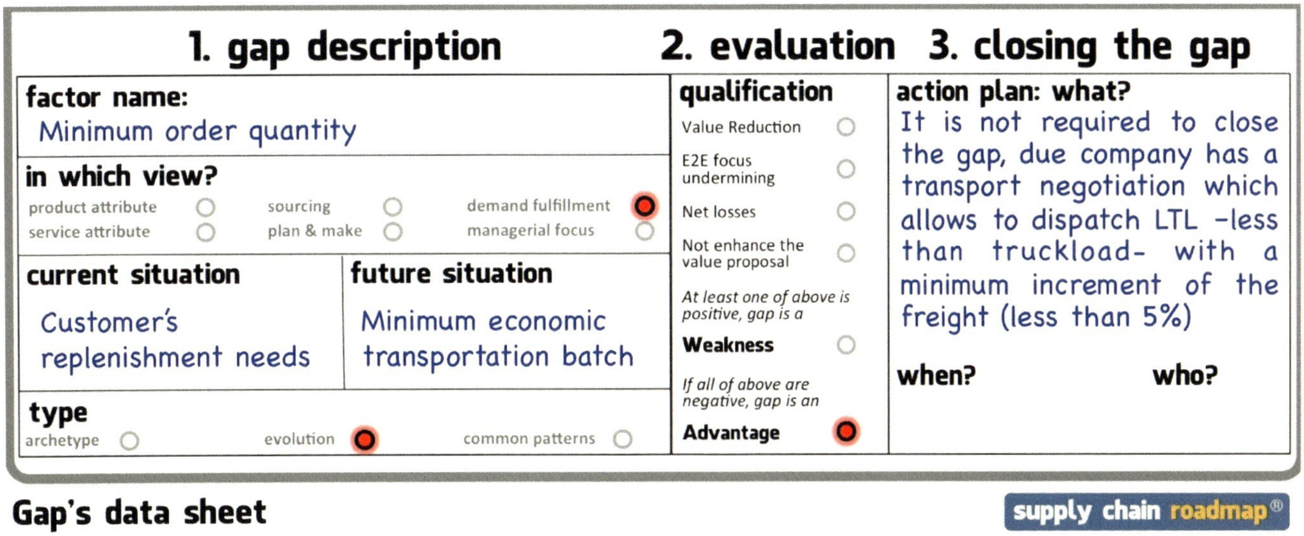

Figure 7.12: Example of Use of Gap Data Sheet

In the next chapter will be presented a real case where is applied the 4-step method.

Chapter 08
Cases

Applying Supply Chain Roadmap in several business scenarios

Applying the Supply Chain Roadmap

The Supply Chain Roadmap can be applied in several business scenarios, as shown in Figure 8.1:

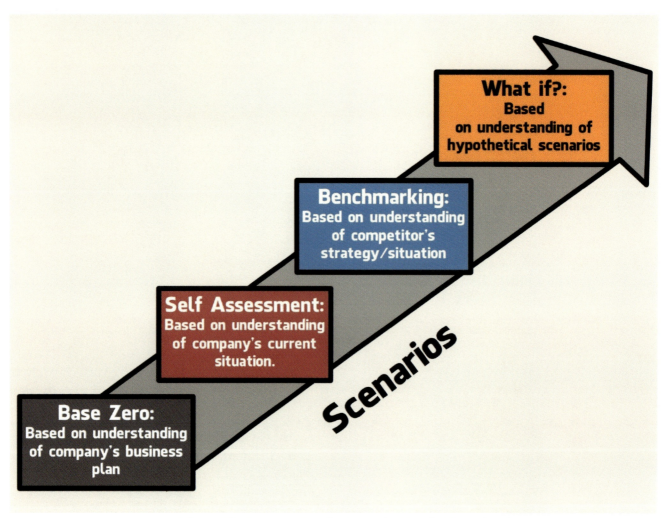

Figure 8.1: Scenarios for Applying the Supply Chain Roadmap

Base Zero: When companies are building a new business, strategy is formulated without having a previous base (i.e., a "base zero" strategy). In this case, strategy is developed based on the information about the Business Framework for the industrial sector and the Unique Value Proposal defined for the organization for the new business. In addition to that, Supply Chain Processes should be defined based on the best-suited Supply Chain Archetype.

Self-Assessment: For "ongoing business," the Supply Chain Roadmap supports the reformulation of the supply chain strategy in order to ensure alignment between supply chain and business strategy.

Benchmarking: In addition to ongoing business, the Supply Chain Roadmap could be used for understanding competitors' strategies and potential failures (gaps) of their strategy that could be exploited in a favorable way.

Taking advantage of these gaps is given by: (1) the enhancement of the value proposition of the company in the attributes for which the competitor has not adequately developed Supply Chain Processes; (2) understand market niches for which the competitor's value proposition is not sufficiently powerful and strengthen relationships with these customers.

For using this approach, the method is applied on the same way explained in Section 5, but the definitions are performed from the perspective of the competitor. Competitors' gaps should be analyzed; based on the findings the UVP could be modified in order to create a greater differentiation under customer's perception.

What if?: The Supply Chain Roadmap could be used for studying "what if?" scenarios in order to be prepared against hypothetical business situations. For using this approach, the method is applied on the same way explained in Section 5, but in the map should be updated the factors source of the hypothetical situation.. For example, if oil prices are too high, transportation cost becomes a relevant issue and the supply chain strategy must consider additional factors that could affect service policies and UVP.

Further, we'll look at a step-by-step assessment of a spun yarn manufacturer, using the Supply Chain Roadmap method. In this example, several tools are used, which is representative of assessments for base zero, self-assessment, and what-if scenarios.

Then we'll look at case studies (Crocs and Tamago-Ya), in order to illustrate how the Supply Chain Roadmap can be used for understanding strategy of companies other than their own (i.e., third parties). This approach is useful for benchmarking current or potential competitors and can be used as teaching tool for understanding of supply chain strategy concepts.

Alpha: A Manufacturer of Intermediate Goods for the Textile Industry

Alpha Company[xiv] is a multinational company headquartered in the United States with operations in countries around the world. Alpha is focused on the manufacture of a very important raw material for the textile industry. Analysis is restricted to one of its factories located in a Latin American country, which is oriented to supply demand into the same country.

Step 1: Segmentation

Alpha produces spun yarn (cotton thread), which is the main raw material for their customers, the majority of which are large textile manufacturers. The product is manufactured in a small quantity of variants (approximately 25 SKUs). Due to homogeneity of products and customers, it is not necessary to segment the supply chain.

Step 2: Understanding

This step aims to characterize the supply chain of Alpha and the industry where Alpha competes.

Cotton thread is a commodity product driven by international prices. Local prices are 5 to 10% higher than international prices, and customers make purchase decisions based on landed cost at their factories. Overseas sourcing (from China and India) is moderately risky due to low to medium delivery reliability and to low service, which manifests in longer order cycles and larger minimum order size requirements than with local suppliers. As a result, customers prefer to maintain a mix of local and imported sourcing.

Despite this, revaluation of the local currency against the dollar has reduced landed cost in local currency of the imported product, increasing preference of local customers for overseas sourcing, which is detrimental for Alpha Company. Figure 8.2 illustrates the current situation of Alpha in the perspectives of Business Framework and UVP.

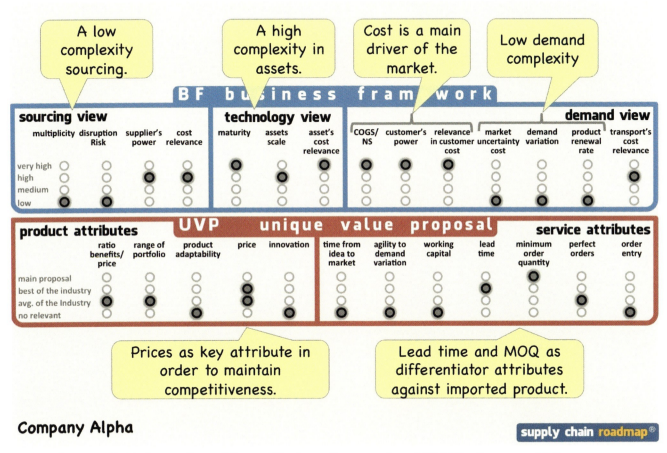

Figure 8.2: Understanding of Current Business Framework and UVP for Company Alpha

Supply Chain Processes are driven by price, which is the key factor in a commoditized industry. Therefore, Alpha is highly oriented to efficiency. However, because Alpha doesn't match landed cost of imported products, the company reduces the production cycle (its production cycle is 15 days long) in order to have smallest batch size. Consequently, Alpha offers the best MOQ (MOQ is LTL less than a truckload, but 80% of the orders are FTL [full truck load]), and, the order cycle is shorter than imported products.

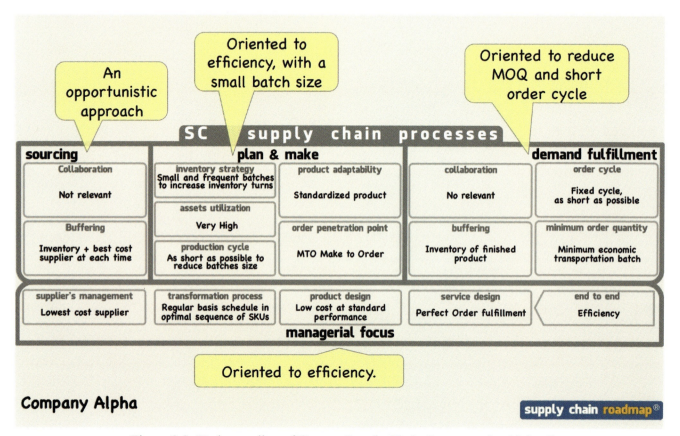

Figure 8.3: Understanding of Current Supply Chain Processes for Alpha Company

The new landscape of the industry, with a local currency revalued, and as consequence of that, customers migrating to imported product, created a major challenge for Alpha. Analysis was focused on finding the gaps between the current situation and the Supply Chain Archetype. The map of Alpha's current supply chain strategy is shown in Figure 8.4.

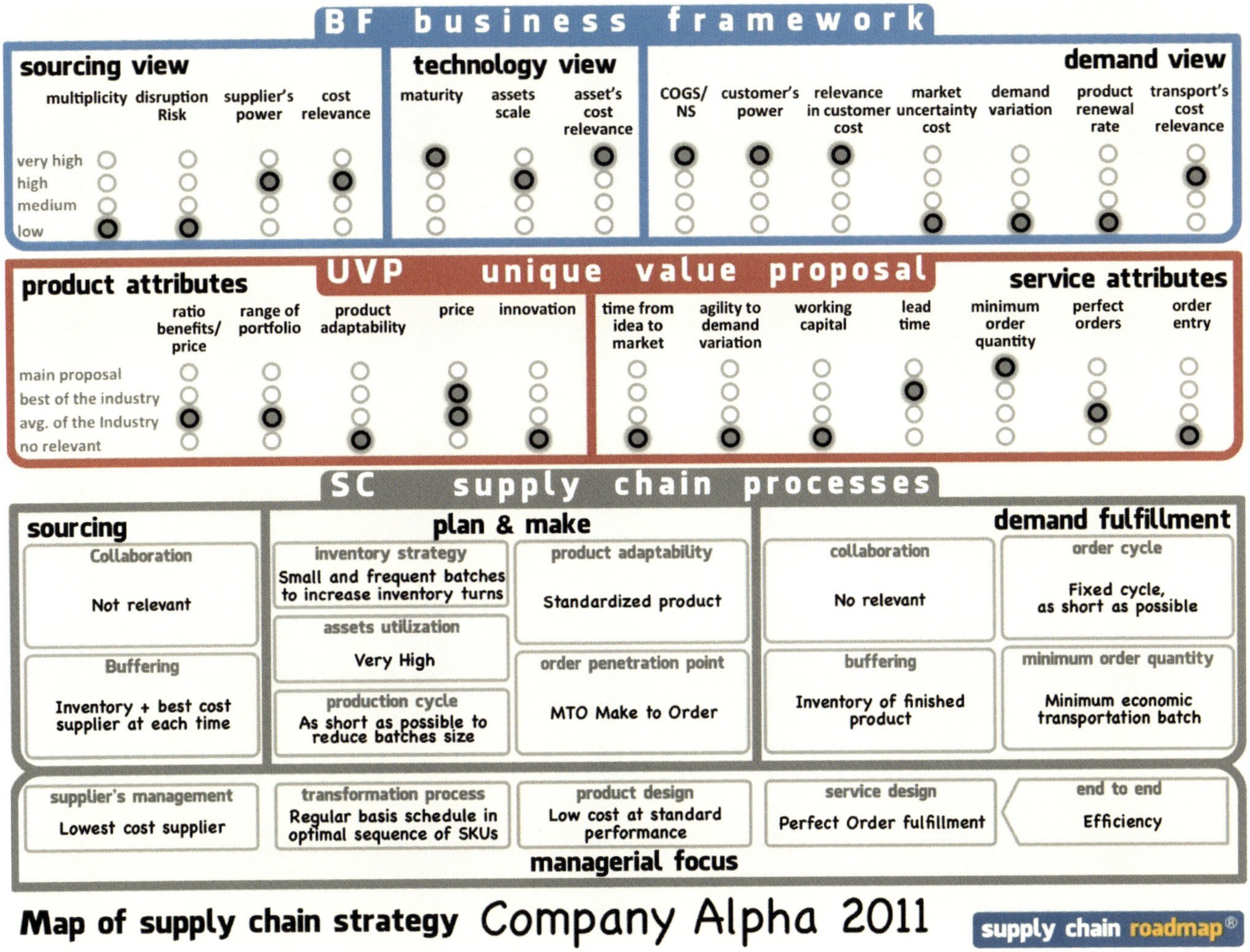

Figure 8.4: Map of Current Supply Chain Strategy for Alpha Company

Step 3: Evaluation

This step is oriented to find the gaps between Alpha's supply chain and the referrals (Best suited Supply Chain Archetype and 10-Common-Patterns).

Alpha's Feasibility Matrix defines a continuous flow supply chain as the best Archetype for its current situation (see Figure 8.5).

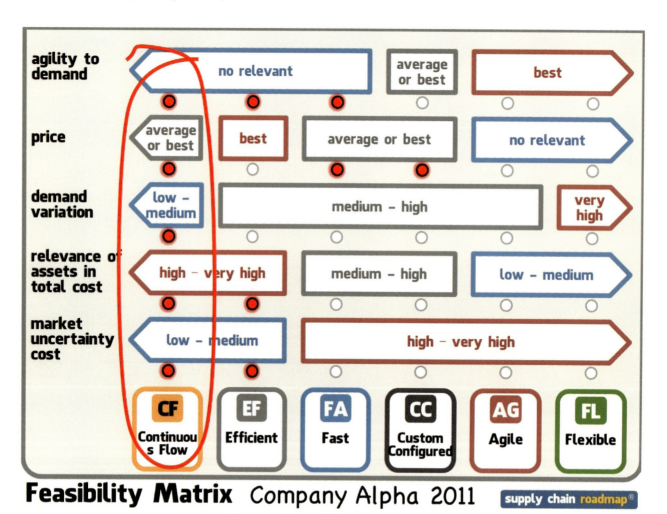

Figure 8.5: Feasibility Matrix for Alpha Company

A comparative analysis between the current supply chain of Alpha and the continuous flow Archetype reveals that the factors of the Business Framework match perfectly and that attributes of the UVP are equal, exception of one, working capital, as is shown in Figure 8.6.

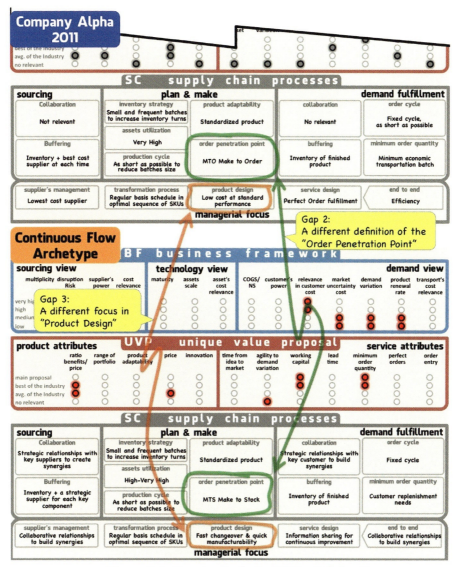

Figure 8.6: Gap Analysis for UVP of Alpha Company

Similarly, a comparative analysis between the supply chain of Alpha and the continuous flow Archetype reveals gaps in six factors of the Supply Chain Processes: OPP, product design focus, service design focus, collaboration, minimum order quantity, and end-to-end focus, as shown in Figures 8.7, and 8.8.

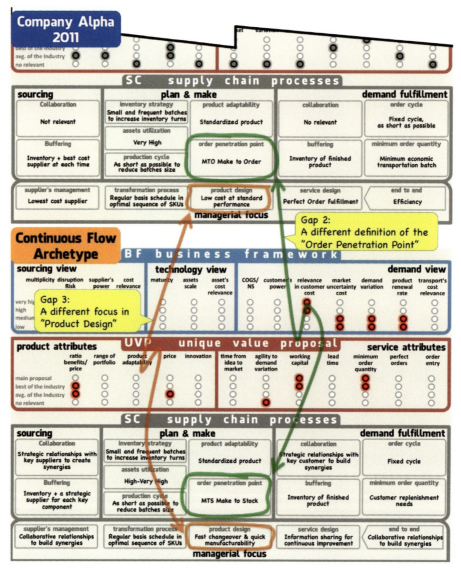

Figure 8.7: Gap Analysis for Supply Chain Processes—Plan & Make—of Alpha Company

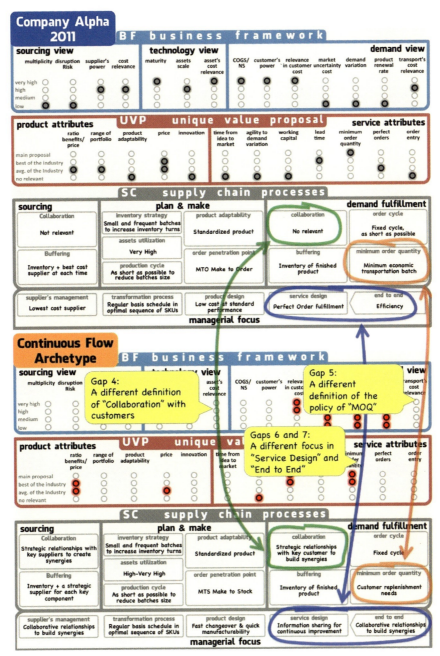

Figure 8.8: Gap Analysis for Supply Chain Processes—Demand Fulfillment—of Alpha Company

Figure 8.9 shows the map of supply chain strategy of Company Alpha, in which the gaps resulting of the comparison with the continuous flow Archetype are highlighted with a red line.

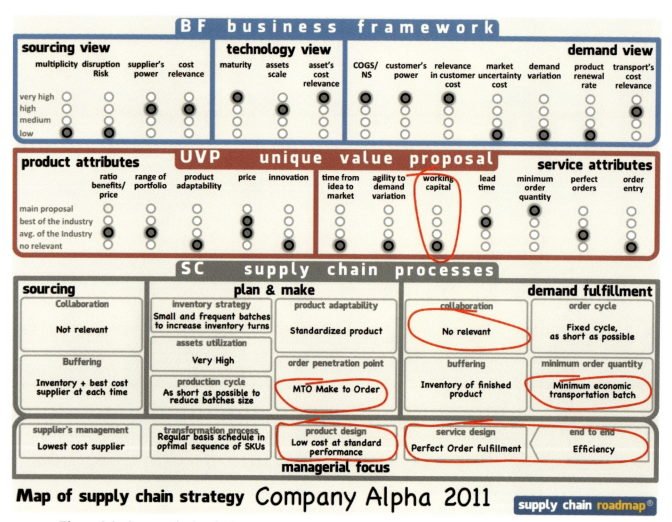

Figure 8.9: Gap Analysis of Alpha Company Against Continuous Flow Archetype

After an analysis of design gaps (i.e., gaps against Supply Chain Archetype) is conducted, compliance gaps (i.e., gaps against Common Patterns) are evaluated. All the Common Patterns are compared against Alpha's supply chain strategy map. Figures 8.10 to 8.14 illustrate the Common Patterns found in the supply chain.

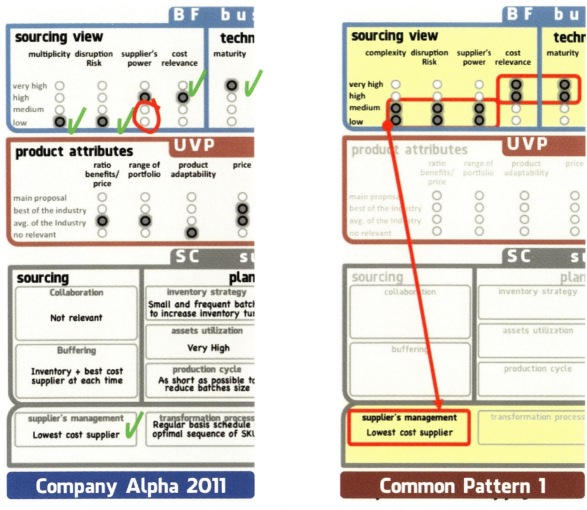

Figure 8.10: Gap Analysis of Common Pattern 1: Industries in a Low Challenging Sourcing

Alpha is in a low challenging sourcing, which resembles the Common Pattern 1 (see Chapter 4), as shown in Figure 8.10. Alpha considered as high the factor of "supplier's power," although this doesn't restrict application of an opportunistic approach for sourcing, because the international market defines cotton price. Consequently, Alpha complies with Common Pattern 2 without gaps.

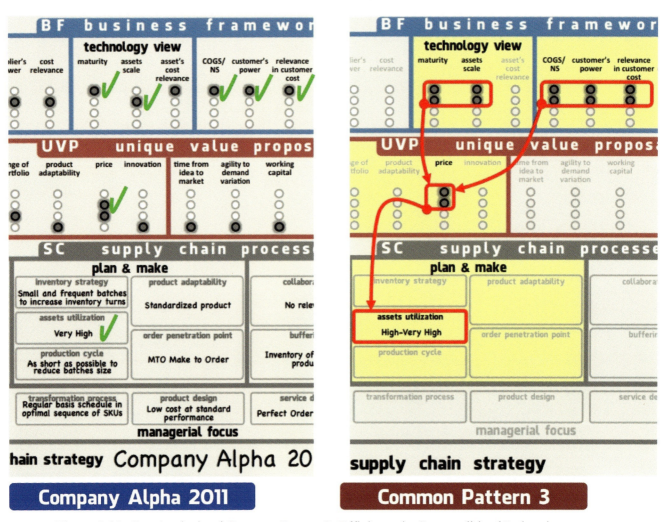

Figure 8.11: Gap Analysis of Common Pattern 3: Efficiency in Commoditized Industries

Alpha complies perfectly Common Pattern 3, as shown in Figure 8.11. Because the industry is commoditized, Alpha should give high importance to asset utilization in order to minimize the relevance of asset cost in the total cost.

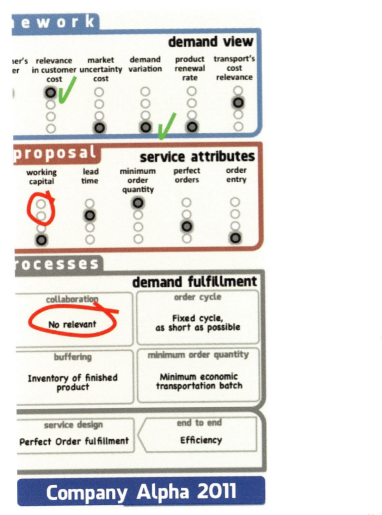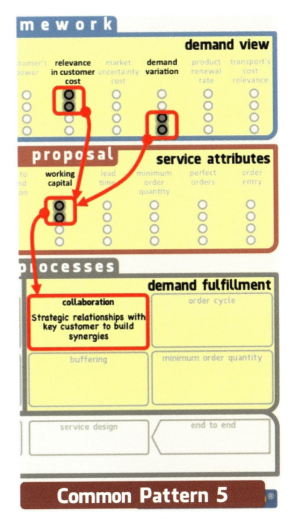

Figure 8.12: Gap Analysis of Common Pattern 5: Collaboration for Optimizing Working Capital

Common Pattern 5 highlights one of the most important gaps for Alpha. Because the product is highly relevant in the customer's cost structure, and because demand variation is high, it is important to offer an optimized working capital for customers. Consequently, it is necessary to develop capabilities in collaboration with customers, as shown in Figure 8.12. It is important to note that both gaps were found in the comparison with the continuous flow Archetype, because they are already considered for the gap analysis.

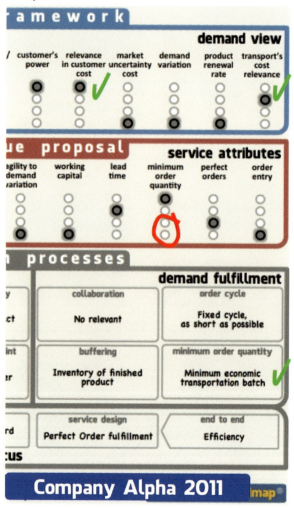
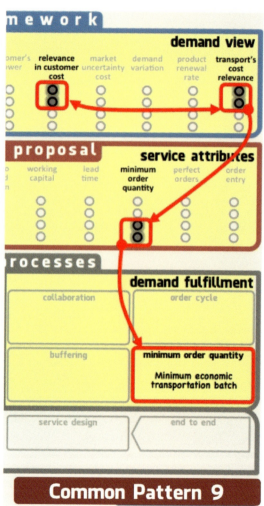

Figure 8.13: Gap Analysis of Common Pattern 9: High Relevance of Transportation Cost

Common Pattern 9 shows an inconsistency of Alpha's strategy. Although Alpha introduces "minimum order quantity" as a key attribute of its strategy, it requires an economic transportation batch as minimum order quantity. Alpha doesn't consider it as a gap, however, because the company allows orders lower than a full truckload (they estimated at least 20% of their orders are below a full truck load), and this policy is considered as the best of the industry. Figure 8.13 analyzes Common Pattern 9.

Step 4: Redesign & Deployment

The last step is oriented to define which gaps should be closed and the action plan for that.

Redesign of the Supply Chain Roadmap for Alpha Company was done using a gap data sheet. Next we look at an evaluation of the gaps and provide an action plan for each one.

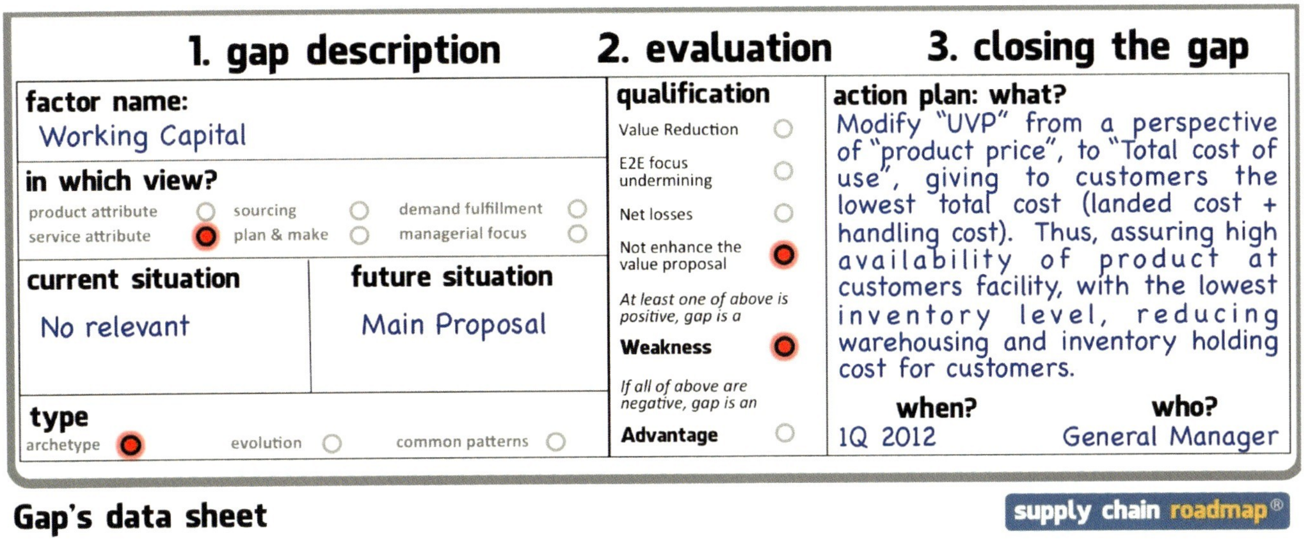

1. gap description

factor name:
Working Capital

in which view?
- product attribute
- service attribute ●
- sourcing
- plan & make ●
- demand fulfillment
- managerial focus

current situation
No relevant

future situation
Main Proposal

type
archetype ●   evolution ○   common patterns ○

2. evaluation

qualification
- Value Reduction ○
- E2E focus undermining ○
- Net losses ○
- Not enhance the value proposal ●

At least one of above is positive, gap is a

- Weakness ●

If all of above are negative, gap is an

- Advantage ○

3. closing the gap

action plan: what?
Modify "UVP" from a perspective of "product price", to "Total cost of use", giving to customers the lowest total cost (landed cost + handling cost). Thus, assuring high availability of product at customers facility, with the lowest inventory level, reducing warehousing and inventory holding cost for customers.

when?   **who?**
1Q 2012   General Manager

Gap's data sheet   supply chain roadmap®

Figure 8.14: Evaluation of Gaps: Working Capital Attribute

Alpha's Supply Chain Roadmap reveals that the company could have a competitive positioning unmatched by their overseas competitors, a UVP based on a competitive price, and differentiation based on offering a continuous replenishment model oriented to ensure product availability, reducing inventory at customer facilities and therefore reducing inventory holding cost in several aspects as warehousing and handling, capital cost, among others. This is summarized in Figure 8.14.

Figure 8.15 illustrates the analysis of the gap of the order penetration point, which, despite a different Archetype, is a competitive advantage for Alpha. This is because using a make-to-order order penetration point ensures a high rate of use of assets, which is supported in an anticipated selling of the productive capacity (generally, they maintain 30 days of production sold).

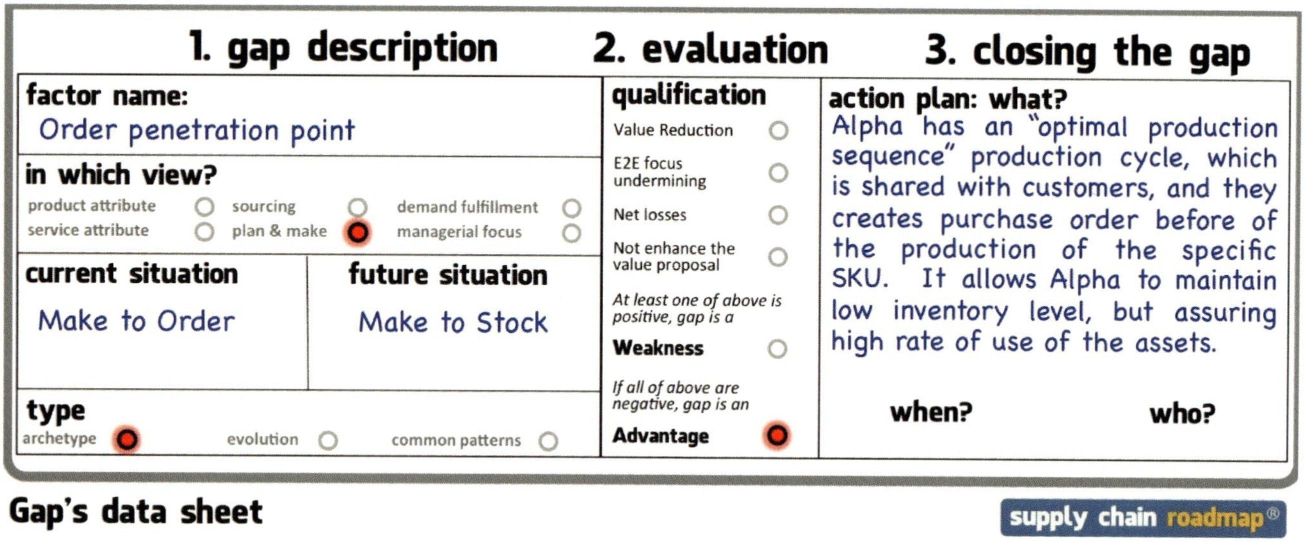

Figure 8.15: Evaluation of Gaps: Order Penetration Point

Figure 8.16 illustrates the analysis of the collaboration gap, which becomes a key capability to be developed by Alpha, in order to offer an optimized working capital at customer facilities. Thus, it is necessary to increase mutual knowledge, specifically when it comes to understanding changes of demand and inventories from the customer's perspective, and to agree upon policies in order to manage inventories level.

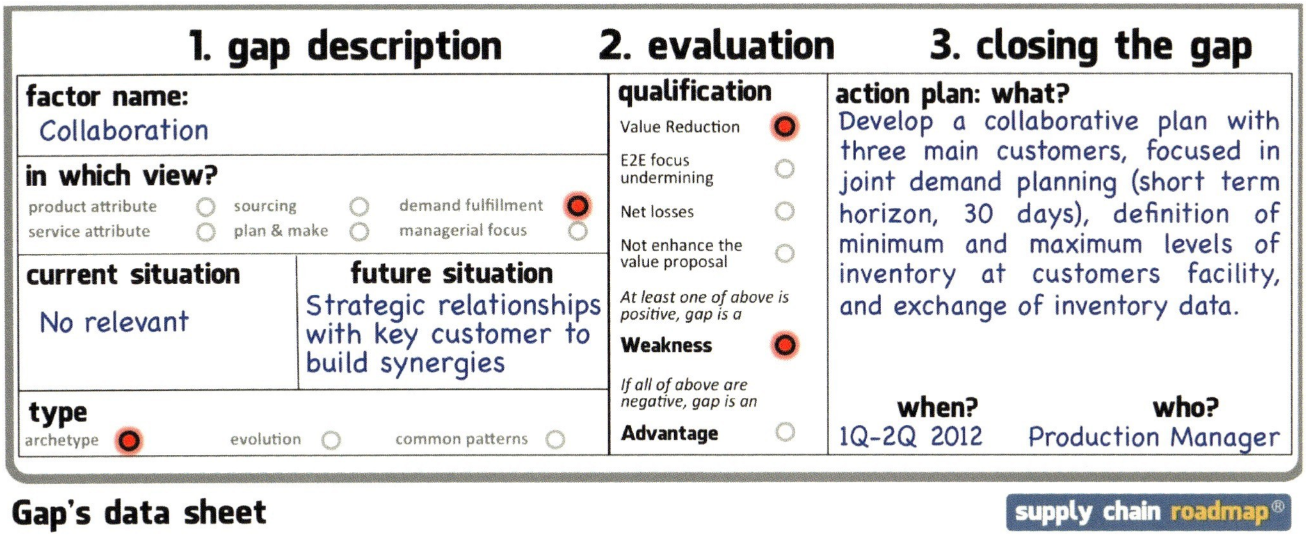

1. gap description		**2. evaluation**	**3. closing the gap**
factor name: Collaboration		**qualification** Value Reduction ●	**action plan: what?** Develop a collaborative plan with three main customers, focused in joint demand planning (short term horizon, 30 days), definition of minimum and maximum levels of inventory at customers facility, and exchange of inventory data.
in which view? product attribute ○ sourcing ○ demand fulfillment ● service attribute ○ plan & make ○ managerial focus ○		E2E focus undermining ○ Net losses ○ Not enhance the value proposal ○	
current situation No relevant	**future situation** Strategic relationships with key customer to build synergies	*At least one of above is positive, gap is a* **Weakness** ●	
type archetype ● evolution ○ common patterns ○		*If all of above are negative, gap is an* **Advantage** ○	**when?** 1Q-2Q 2012 **who?** Production Manager

Gap's data sheet   supply chain roadmap®

Figure 8.16: Evaluation of Gaps: Collaboration

Consolidating action plans, the main recommendations for Alpha were:
- Maintain "efficiency oriented" upstream supply chain in order to ensure a minimum price gap against international competitors.
- Complement UVP in service from minimum order quantity with low working capital, which ensures an Order Winner Attribute under customer perspective -as was defined previously, an OrderWinner Attribute is an attribute with high differentiation with respect to competitors and allows "win" most customer orders than competitors-.
- Increase tactical actions in order to develop deep collaborative relationships with customers seeking to enhance low working capital and low risk supplier features.

Tactical actions should be oriented to enhance low working capital by four actions:
- Reduce working capital.
- Increase delivery frequency and collaborative planning in order to reduce customer's inventory, inclusive of offering vendor management inventory programs to customers.
- Increase working capital value perception.

- Estimate product total cost (landed cost + inventory handling + inventory holding cost + financial cost), in order to give relevance of these costs to customers.

Results

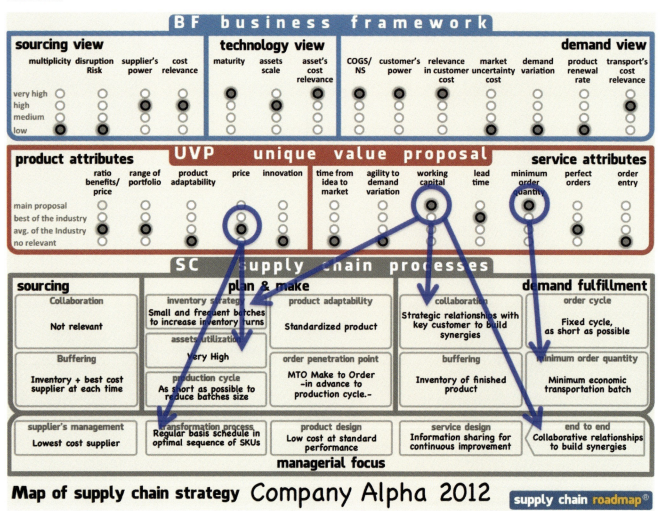

Figure 8.17: Map of Alpha's New Supply Chain Strategy

The Supply Chain Roadmap generated a change in the managerial focus of Alpha, moving from a perspective mainly oriented to low cost and efficiency to a perspective oriented to a continuous replenishment to customers in order to optimize working capital on customers, based on the capability that had made them successful: an efficient supply chain.

After the Supply Chain Roadmap assessment, Alpha introduced a continuous replenishment model based on the tactical principles of the buffers management of the Theory of Constraints[xv].

This approach allowed Alpha to: (1) offer the lowest total cost for the customer, based on a competitive product price enhanced with and optimized working capital management; (2) preserve its market share, ensuring a high rate of use of assets and, therefore, positive financial results.

Figure 8.17 shows the three core elements of Alpha's Unique Value Proposal: competitive price, low working capital, and the lowest minimum order quantity of the industry. It also illustrates the factors of the Supply Chain Processes supporting them.

CROCS: When Strategy and Implementation Are Misaligned [xvi] [xvii]

A common mistake companies make is to formulate a great strategy but then gradually move away from it when it is actually being deployed, thus implementing a strategy with serious inconsistencies.

A good example of above is the case of Crocs in the period 2006–08. The famous shoe manufacturer's supply chain strategy was documented in a case developed by Stanford University in 2007, which explained the evolution of Crocs's supply chain and the strategy behind it. The gradual deviation of the strategy led to large inconsistencies in the company's supply chain, which reflected negatively during 2008.

In an industry characterized for low responsiveness to demand, and where retailers and distributors are obliged to create purchase orders eight or more months in advance of the sales season, Crocs developed a supply chain strategy oriented to satisfy changes in demand during the same sales season, which was something never before seen in the industry.

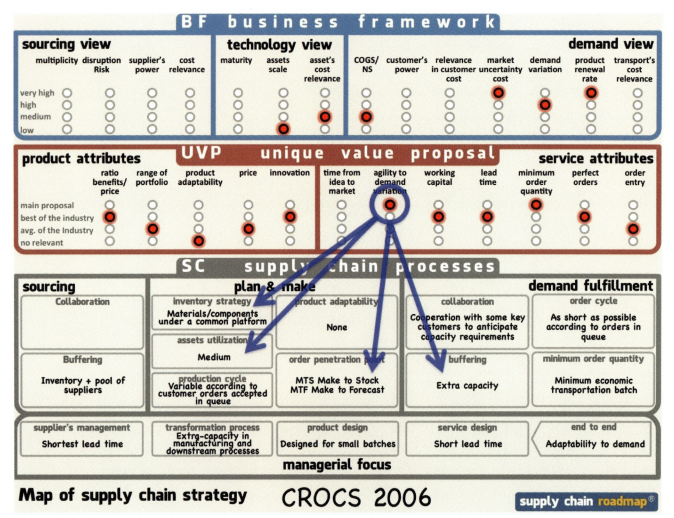

Figure 8.18: Map of Formulated Supply Chain Strategy of Crocs in 2006

Figure 8.18 shows the map of supply chain strategy of Crocs, according to the description realized in the Stanford case study and Crocs's annual report to investors. Crocs backed this proposal in an agile supply chain, which had an extra-capacity of one million pairs of shoes per month beyond the actual production plan. In its 2006 annual report, Crocs explained this strategy:

"We believe our in-house manufacturing capabilities enable us to rapidly make changes to production, providing us with the flexibility to quickly respond to orders for high-demand models and colors throughout the year, while outsourcing allows us to capitalize on the efficiencies and cost benefits of using contract manufacturing. We believe that this production strategy will enable us to continue to minimize our production costs and increase overall operating efficiencies as well as shorten production and development times to better serve our retail customers."

Despite this, deployment of Crocs's supply chain strategy was very different from the formulated strategy. A detailed analysis of its financial statements reported a high level of inventory—204 days at the end of 2006, and 259 days at the end of 2007—mainly concentrated in finished product, which is not aligned with its agile strategy. Worse, a high level of inventory is not adequate for a business oriented to fashion, with a high market uncertainty cost.

In its 2007 report, Crocs justified its approach by its rapid growth, which was more than 2.4 times from 2006 to 2007. However, in 2008, Crocs recognized its mistake in the management of the supply chain, as was explained in the annual report of 2008: "a write-down of inventories relates to certain products that were or are going to be discontinued of $76.3 million, including core products in colors that have experienced substantial declines in consumer demand."

In addition, Crocs reduced its production capacity in order to adjust its cost structure to decreased demand and declining revenues.

Using Supply Chain Roadmap analysis, Crocs revealed a critical gap against the agile Supply Chain Archetype: Inventory strategy for an agile supply chain is oriented to maintain inventory of materials and components under a common platform, in the case of Crocs, the crosslite material –*the main raw material of their shoes*-. Crocs, however, moved to having a high level of inventory of finished product, a strategy more adequate for industries in a Business Framework of low market uncertainty cost. This high level of finished product was the root cause of the Crocs's issues, the inventory became obsolete as a result of changes in fashion trends. This proved to be an example of erroneous management of a supply chain with high level of market uncertainty cost.

Today, Crocs is a successful company. In 2011, the company reported a change in its strategy, providing incentives to customers in order to produce in advance of each season, as is explained in the annual report: "We receive a significant portion of orders as preseason orders, generally four to six months prior to shipment date. We provide customers with price incentives to participate in such preseason programs to enable us to better plan our production schedule, inventory and shipping needs."

This change in strategy—moving from an fully agile supply chain to a mixed supply chain of agile and efficient—allowed Crocs to report in their financial statements 101 days of inventory, practically a third of what the company reported in 2007.

Tamago Ya: When a Focused Supply Chain Creates an Unmatched Value Proposal [xviii] [xix]

When supply chain strategy is coherent and focused, the UVP is highly differentiated against competitors. An example is the case of Tamago-Ya, a delivery of lunch boxes for office workers in Tokyo - Japan, which was studied by Stanford University. In this case study, we can see the power of the UVP when the supply chain strategy is fully focused.

Tamago-Ya produced and delivered high-quality lunch boxes at low prices to office workers in the Tokyo metropolitan area, competing against other delivery services, fast food restaurants, and convenience restaurants located near to the most populated offices zone of Tokyo.

Tamago-Ya's UVP was characterized by:
- Offered a unique option in its menu of the day, although menu was changed in a daily basis.
- A high-quality menu featuring organic and natural ingredients.
- Orders are received from 9 am to 10:30 am, and delivered at noon.

A typical delivery van could carry 250 lunch boxes, but Tamago-Ya owned a proprietary design of the lunch box, which allowed them to carry 430 lunch boxes in a van without reducing the amount of food in each lunch box compared against competitors.

The cost of producing a lunch box by Tamago-Ya was higher than industry average, by more than 20%.

New customers were accepted under two main criteria: At least 10 lunch boxes per order, and the customer should be located in the same building of another customer or located along an existing delivery route.

Several aspects characterized Tamago-Ya's supply chain:

- A closer relationship among van drivers and customers, based on face-to-face contact when van drivers delivered the lunch boxes and on feedback received when the van drivers retrieved the reusable boxes. (In contrast to the industry, which used disposable boxes, Tamago-Ya used reusable boxes, which was slightly more expensive than disposable boxes, but allowed a better appeal of the lunch and a permanent feedback of the customers.)
- Van drivers predicted how many order would be placed on their own distribution route for the next day, based on the customer feedback.
- Production was based on a make-to-forecast order penetration point, based on the company's own forecasts and adjusted according to orders received before noon.
- Production facilities were located near suppliers in order to have higher delivery speed in case of unexpected demand, which also allowed for maintaining zero inventory. Tamago-Ya only kept inventory of sauces and condiments; fresh components were requested on demand.
- Customer zones far away from the production facility were dispatched before the nearest zones, and stand-by vans were used to adjust delivery to real demand.

Figure 8.19 shows the map of supply chain strategy of Tamago-Ya. The company employed a strategy based on a single daily menu, which became in the core of its supply chain—an efficient supply chain reinforced with concepts of other Archetypes:

The company's main competitive advantage was to eliminate the market uncertainty cost generated by lost sales or expired product, transforming the most difficult condition of the Business Framework for the industry in his core competence. Market uncertainty cost was eliminated by the implementation of a unique menu per day and collaborative demand planning, thereby reducing customer choices to two options—request or no request a delivery—and reducing the uncertainty associated with customers choice through the collaborative planning performed by the truck drivers.

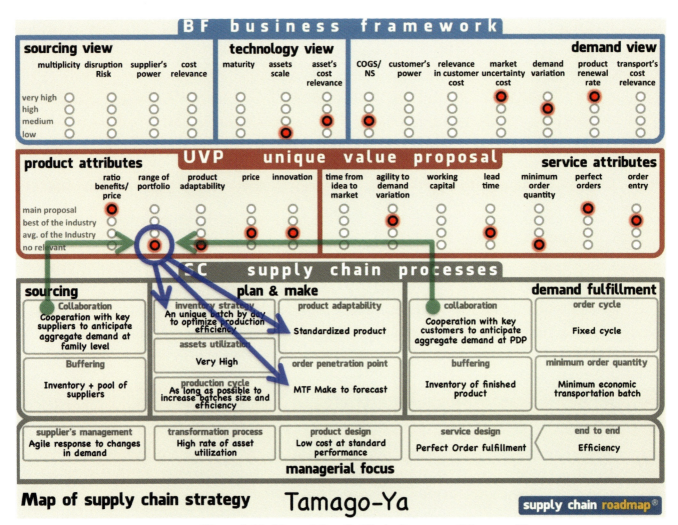

Figure 8.19: Map of Supply Chain Strategy of Tamago-Ya

Other important factors of the Tamago-Ya's supply chain are:
- The unique daily menu became a source of productivity: a larger production batch than competitors offering menus with multiple dishes.

- The "10 boxes by delivery along the delivery routes" rule, combined with a higher carrying capacity, became a source of lower distribution costs.
- A strong collaborative relationship with customers, in order to anticipate demand and receive feedback of the service.
- A closer relationship with suppliers, oriented to have an agile sourcing of fresh foods to satisfy demand variation.

These factors are a source of cost efficiency, which Tamago-Ya takes advantage of in order to offer a higher quality product than its competitors, providing their customers an unmatched UVP. The company created a new value proposal, which is positioned among the two most predominant market proposals (fast food/home cooking restaurants, or, packaged food as is usual in convenience retailers as 7-Eleven), providing the most valuable features of both: fresh food in the case of fast food/home cooking restaurants, and fast service, without waiting lines, in the case of packaged foods.

Tamago-ya's case is an example of the importance of the alignment between Business Framework and supply chain strategy. The company employs a pioneering supply chain strategy that succeeds because of a coherent strategy in which sources of misalignment are eliminated (i.e., demand uncertainty and high market mediation cost) by an innovative approach (see Figure 8.19).

Outlook

Supply Chain Roadmap ® is the result of several years of experience as a supply chain professional and as a professor and speaker in supply chain management. The method is in continuous evolution, and the contributions of people from several countries around the world have been compiled in this version.

The most important goal of the book is to make available to students *–undergraduate, graduate, and executive education-*, professors, consultants, supply chain professionals, and, in general, industrial organizations, a method that allows the connection between supply chain theory and the practice of the supply chain management, allowing the alignment from supply chain with business strategy.

Comments or suggestions for improving the Supply Chain Roadmap ® method are welcome. Please share your thoughts with hdperez@supplychainroadmap.com, and visiting www.SupplyChainRoadmap.com.

About the author

Hernan David Perez is the creator of Supply Chain Roadmap ® method, he has developed the method as result of his experience in supply chain management in several fields such as professor of postgraduate students, speaker in supply chain strategy, and, his real experience in management positions in the supply chain in multinational companies in several sectors such as automotive, FMCG -fast moving consumer goods-, B2B, and retail.

Born in Medellin-Colombia, Hernan David has a Bachelor degree in Mechanical Engineering of Universidad Pontificia Boliviariana, a Diploma in Production and Services Management of Escuela de Ingenieria de Antioquia, a Master in Operations Management of Universidad de la Sabana, and, a Certification in Supply Chain Management of Massachusetts Institute of Technology –MIT-.

Notes and references

[i] Laseter Tim, Oliver Keith. "When will supply chain management grow up?". Strategy + Business, Fall 2003, 32.
[ii] Porter, Michael. "Competitive advantage". The Free Press. 1985.
[iii] Mentzer, Jhon. et.al. "Defining Supply Chain Management" Journal of Business Logistics, Vol 22, No 2, 2001.
[iv] PORTER, Michael. Competitive strategy. Free Press, 1980.
[v] Skinner, Wickham. "The productivity paradox". Harvard Business Review, July-August 1986.
[vi] HILL, Alex. HILL Terry. Manufacturing Operations Strategy. 3rd Edition, Palgrave, 2009.
[vii] FISHER, Marshall. What is the right supply chain for your product?. Harvard Business Review. Mar-Apr 1997.
[viii] CHRISTOPHER, Martin. The agile supply chain. Industrial Marketing Management 29, 37–44 (2000). CHRISTOPHER, Martin. "A taxonomy for selecting global supply chain strategies". The International Journal of Logistics Management Vol. 17 No. 2, 2006 pp. 277-287
[ix] LEE, Hau. Aligning supply chain strategies with product uncertainties. California Management Review. Volume 44, Number 3, Spring 2002. p. 105-119.
[x] CHRISTOPHER, Martin. GATTORNA John. Supply chain cost management and value-based pricing. Industrial marketing management. 34 (2005) p. 115-121.
[xi] GATTORNA, Jhon. Cadenas de abastecimiento dinámicas. Bogotá: Ediciones ECOE, 2009. p. 37.
[xii] KETCHEN, David. HULT, Tomas. Bridging organization theory and supply chain management: the case of best value supply chains. Journal of operations management. 25 (2007) 573-580.
[xiii] Some excerpts and figures of the book are taken from the article "Supply Chain Strategies: Which one hits the mark?" by Hernan David Perez. Copyright 2013 by CSCMP's Supply Chain Quarterly www.SupplyChainQuarterly.com, a division of Supply Chain Media LLC. Reprinted with permission.
[xiv] For confidentiality reasons real name of the Company under assessment has been changed to Alpha company.
[xv] See details about buffers management in "Theory of Constraints Handbook" by James Cox III and John Schleier.
[xvi] Analysis of the CROCS case as basis for example of use of Supply Chain Roadmap method, rather than to illustrate either effective or ineffective handling of an administrative situation.
[xvii] Analysis of CROCS based on the case CROCS: REVOLUTIONIZING AN INDUSTRY'S SUPPLY CHAIN MODEL FOR COMPETITIVE ADVANTAGE –University of Stanford", and, Crocs' annual reports to stockholders (Form 10-K) -2006, 2007, 2008, 2011-.
[xviii] Analysis of the TAMAGO-YA case as basis for example of use of Supply Chain Roadmap method, rather than to illustrate either effective or ineffective handling of an administrative situation.
[xix] Analysis of TAMAGO-YA based on the case TAMAGO-YA OF JAPAN: DELIVERING LUNCH BOXES TO YOUR WORK – University of Stanford.

CPSIA information can be obtained
at www.ICGtesting.com
Printed in the USA
LVIC04n0023130314
377217LV00002B/3